Date Due

NOV 20 '89

THE GREAT
TRIBULATION

WHAT THE
BIBLE SAYS
ABOUT
THE GREAT
TRIBULATION

William R. Kimball

BAKER BOOK HOUSE
Grand Rapids, Michigan 49506

to

My wife Rose,
And my daughters Angela and Rachel,

Without whose understanding
and loving support,

This work would not have
been possible.

with special thanks

to

Linda Murley for her countless hours
of secretarial assistance, to Ken for his
creative contribution in illustrating this
book, and to an innumerable company
of unnamed saints who have helped
make this endeavor a reality.

Art by Ken Norberg

For several years, Ken worked as a graphic artist
and illustrator. He left his position in commercial
art in reponse to God's call to Christian service,
and now resides in Kalamazoo, Michigan, where
he serves a church.

v

Table of Contents

Preface

Tensions in the Mid-East, the threat of nuclear holocaust, the escalating arms race, economic uncertainty, global instability—a token of things to come? One has only to consider the present world condition to wonder whether we are nearing the end. Are the *signs of the times* pointing to a final period of unprecedented chaos referred to in the Bible as the *Great Tribulation*? Many Christians are absolutely convinced that the storm clouds are now gathering for this catastrophic event. Their belief is based upon strong appeals to the scriptures, especially those statements spoken by Christ in the Mount Olivet prophecy. They claim that such passages as:

> For then shall be *great tribulation* such as was not since the beginning of the world to this time, no, nor ever shall be (Matthew 24:21).

give unquestionable support to their perspective of the future.

But is this belief justified? Do the scriptures support this perspective? Does the Olivet prophecy really teach that this age will end in a final period of cataclysmic upheaval known as the *Great Tribulation*? Did Jesus actually characterize the last days as those of such unparalleled calamity that they will dwarf anything in history? These are timely and provocative questions for each of us to consider.

These are not, however, new questions. The church has struggled with these problems for centuries. In fact, these very questions are what prompted Christ to deliver His prophetic appraisal of the church age on the Mount of Olives. This book endeavors to answer these questions. It does so by going to the source. It does so by exploring Christ's personal response to these questions contained in the greatest of all Bible prophecies—the Mount Olivet discourse.

ix

One of the primary objectives of this book is to challenge the myth of a future *Great Tribulation*. It does so by examining the very proof passages which supposedly support this teaching. It proves that Christ's prophetic appraisal of the church age lends little support to this popular position. It shows that the actual conditions of the last days are radically opposed to those so frequently sensationalized by prophetic speculators today, and it considers the resulting consequences and implications for the church.

This work, while not attempting to represent an exhaustive treatment of every major area of prophetic controversy, does endeavor to reflect as sound and comprehensive a treatment of Christ's Olivet prophecy as possible. It offers a balanced evaluation of the great tribulation, the timing of Christ's return, the prevailing conditions of the last days, and the unique tests and perils facing the church. In so doing, it provides Christians with the essential insights and understanding needed to victoriously encounter the challenges of the future.

In conclusion, I'm aware that some readers will find this book disturbing; some may view it as a threat; some will strongly reject it; and others will conveniently dismiss it on the grounds of prophetic incompatibility. But regardless of our response, may we each consider the wise and timely admonition of the Apostle Paul to "Prove all things, (and) hold fast to that which is good" (I Thessalonians 5:21). It may be that some will discover this work to be a refreshing and rewarding contribution to the field of prophetic inquiry.

THE GREAT
TRIBULATION

The Late Great Tribulation

Introduction

The Mount Olivet prophecy is recorded in each of the synoptic gospels, the most familiar of which is found in Matthew. Each account begins as the Lord and His apostolic band were departing the temple compound in the aftermath of Christ's most intensive denunciation against the Jewish authorities (Matthew 23). As they made their way through the shadows of the temple structure, some of the disciples, being awestruck by the grandeur of the temple and the enormous masonry used in its construction, drew the Lord's attention to the impressive beauty and architectural solidity of the building. But as the disciples "spoke of the temple, (and) how it was adorned with goodly stones and gifts" (Luke 21:5), Jesus stunned them with the sobering declaration that it would one day be reduced to rubble:

MATT. 24	MARK 13	LUKE 21
2 And Jesus said unto them, See ye not all these things? verily I say unto you, There shall not be left here one stone upon another, that shall not be thrown down.	2 And Jesus answering said unto him, Seest thou these great buildings? there shall not be left one stone upon another, that shall not be thrown down.	6 As for these things which ye behold, the days will come, in the which there shall not be left one stone upon another, that shall not be thrown down.

It was this startling revelation which set the stage for the Olivet prophecy.

A short time later, as they rested upon the Mount of Olives overlooking the city of Jerusalem, a delegation of His disciples approached Him privately concerning the brief but electrifying news He had just spoken. His earlier comments had produced a deep perplexity in the disciples and prompted them to seek out a more comprehensive explanation of Christ's astonishing revelation concerning the temple's destruction. They further requested Him to elaborate upon the sign of His coming and the end of the world. His response to these questions resulted in the Mount Olivet prophecy.

The Mt. Olivet discourse is the most important prophecy in the Bible, for it represents Christ's personal appraisal of the church age. It is the great pivotal prophecy upon which many teachings either stand or fall. An accurate interpretation of this crucial prophecy provides us with an invaluable, foundational framework for establishing solid prophetic positions. A sound interpretation supplies us with a balanced counterweight to prophetic extremism, and gives us a reliable set of guidelines to counter many of the misleading interpretations which often accompany other related passages. In short, Christ's prophetic comments contain numerous checks and balances against prophetic misrepresentation.

A wrong interpretation of this prophecy has often resulted in a multitude of erroneous concepts, foolish theorizing, and fanciful speculations concerning the prophetic forecasts of the future. Like the "domino principle," when the Olivet discourse is pushed out of balance, all related prophecies down the line are subsequently knocked out of alignment. It is my opinion that this has been a common occurrence when approaching the truths contained within this prophecy.

The main reasons for the numerous errors found in various interpretations of the Olivet prophecy lie fundamentally in, 1) a failure to accurately establish the exact context and application of the key divisions of the discourse, and, 2) in the bias of expositors who have been overly influenced by established prophetic systems, speculations, and timetables. The pattern of forcing the scriptures to bow before the "sacred cows" of prophetic tradition has often been the case when interpreting the Olivet discourse. Because the priority in interpreting has often been placed upon a prophetic system rather than upon the clear thrust of the Word, there has been a common reluctance to accept the scriptures at

2

face value or in the proper contextual setting which the Lord intended to convey. The result has often been baneful to the study of prophecy. This work represents a reversal of this common pattern. It is an endeavor to present as clear and unbiased an interpretation of Christ's prophetic words as possible, and to do contextual justice to the intended meaning, application, and timing of the Lord's statements.

The Prophecy in Context

No scripture is spoken in a vacuum. Every passage must be viewed in the light not only of its immediate context, but in the broader context of the book in which it is located, as well as the Bible as a whole. The Mt. Olivet discourse is no exception. It is not an isolated prophecy, but represents the accumulative product of many prophecies and warnings delivered to the Jewish nation. To properly establish the contextual framework for interpreting this prophecy, we must first examine the immediate setting preceding the important statements Jesus provided His disciples as they were leaving the temple compound (Matthew 24:2).

The Olivet discourse was delivered shortly after Christ made His triumphant entry into Jerusalem. His messianic mission was rapidly approaching its climax. He had already purged the temple of the moneychangers and had enraged His Jewish adversaries through an intensive series of heated confrontations. The behind-the-scenes plotting for His life was gaining momentum as the flames of contention increased between Him and the religious authorities.

Matthew 23 records Christ's longest, most scathing rebuke against the hypocrisy and wickedness of the Jewish leaders. He concluded His awesome impeachment with these words:

Wherefore ye be witnesses unto yourselves, that ye are the children of them which killed the prophets. Fill ye up then the measure of your fathers. Ye serpents, ye generation of vipers, how can ye escape the damnation of hell? Verily I say unto you, All these things shall come upon this generation (Matthew 23:31-33, 36).

The significance of these words and their immediate bearing upon the context of the Olivet discourse cannot be minimized. His condemnation clearly indicated the divine retribution which was awaiting that generation of Jews: "Ye serpents, ye generation of vipers, how can ye escape the damnation of hell? Verily I say unto you, ALL THESE THINGS SHALL COME UPON THIS GENERATION" (Matthew 23:33, 36). His words served as the final, judicial sentence against the Jewish nation as He categorizes the crimes for which that generation would be punished.

Their national sin had been accumulating for centuries. By sentencing their Messiah to death, and persecuting His servants, they were proving themselves to be the children of those who had murdered the prophets. They were following faithfully in the infamous footsteps of their forefathers. They were filling up the full measure of wrath (Matthew 23:32) for which they would be repaid by the terrible retribution of God. His words echoed the earlier warnings of John the Baptist who challenged the same religious authorities, "O generation of vipers, who hath warned you to flee from the wrath to come?" (Matthew 3:7b).

In concluding His divine verdict, Jesus added a tragic lamentation:

O Jerusalem, Jerusalem, thou that killest the prophets, and stonest them which are sent unto thee, how often would I have gathered thy children together, even as a hen gathereth her chickens under her wings, and ye would not! Behold, your house is left unto you desolate. For I say unto you, Ye shall not see me henceforth, till ye shall say, Blessed is he that cometh in the name of the Lord (Matthew 23:37-39; see also Luke 13:34, 35).

This grim pronouncement clearly warned of the doom which was about to befall that city. In essence, Christ's sobering declaration, *and ye would not,* served as a fitting epitaph for the rebellious nation of Israel.

However, these were not the only warnings of impending judgment. A few days earlier, as He approached Jerusalem for His triumphant entry, He paused, overlooking the city, and wept over it (Luke 19:41). Although He was soon destined to face His own personal agonies, rejection, and humiliation at the hands of the Jews, He was deeply moved to anguish as He considered the holocaust awaiting the Jewish nation:

And when he was come near, he beheld the city, and wept over it, saying, If thou hadst known, even thou, at least in this thy day, the things which belong unto thy peace! but now they are hid from thine eyes. For the days shall come upon thee, that thine enemies shall cast a trench about thee, and compass thee round, and keep thee in on every side, and *shall lay thee even with the ground, and thy children within thee; and they shall not leave in thee one stone upon another; because thou knewest not the time of thy visitation* (Luke 19:41-44).

His remorseful words provide us with an accurate prediction of the punishment which was destined to befall the beloved city of Jerusalem. The issue of the city's impending destruction held a position of extreme significance to the Lord because of its historical impact upon the Jewish nation, the exhaustive nature of the judgment, the intensity of the atrocities accompanying it, and the resulting consequences to the entire world.

After His triumphant entrance into the city, Christ delivered a series of parables which characterized the nation's obstinate refusal to embrace their Messiah. In the parable of the marriage of the king's son (Matthew 22:1-4), Jesus prophetically foreshadowed the fate of the Jews for rejecting the gracious invitation of God to partake in the wedding festivities of His Son. His parabolic statements served as an apt warning of things to come:

> But when the king heard thereof, he was wroth and he sent forth his armies, and destroyed those murderers, and burned up their city (Matthew 22:7).

A few days later, as He was being led out of the city to be crucified, a great company of people along the route wept and sorrowed over His sentence. The grief of the women moved Him to draw their attention to the approaching calamities which would eventually engulf the city and bring unparalleled suffering upon them:

> But Jesus turning unto them said, Daughters of Jerusalem, weep not for me, but weep for yourselves, and for your children. For, behold, the days are coming, in the which they shall say, Blessed are the barren, and the wombs that never bare, and the paps which never gave suck. Then shall they begin to say to the mountains, Fall on us; and to the hills, Cover us. For if they do these things in a green tree, what shall be done in the dry? (Luke 23:28-31).

Even in Christ's personal hour of anguish, He revealed that the sufferings which awaited the Jewish nation were of a far greater severity than those which He was called to endure.

Correcting a Misconception

Christ's parting words to His Jewish adversaries, coupled with the startling revelation of Jerusalem's awaiting judgment, indicated two essential things to His followers:

1. A catastrophic judgment was soon destined to befall that generation of Jews resulting in the utter ruin of their sacred temple: "Behold, your house is left unto you desolate" (Matthew 23:38); "Verily I say unto you, All these things shall come upon this generation" (Matthew 23:36).

and,

2. In consummating His stern reproof He had revealed that He would visibly return and, at that time, the Jews would openly receive Him with rejoicing. This latter event was intimated with the words, "Ye shall not see me henceforth, till ye shall say, Blessed is he that cometh in the name of the Lord" (Matthew 23:39).

Both of these thoughts were fresh in the disciples' thinking when they approached Christ for a fuller explanation of these matters to which He had only briefly referred. It was His earlier statements involving Jerusalem's impending destruction and the announcement of His visible return which accounts for the form of the questions presented by His disciples:

> Tell us, when shall these things be? (the timing of Jerusalem's ruin) and what shall be the sign of thy coming, and of the end of the world? (the thought of His return) (Matthew 24:3b).

The manner in which the disciples combined these questions reveals that they were not simply presenting different questions involving several distinct and unrelated events, but were essentially asking what, to them, was a series of closely inter-related events. This is implied by the form of their questions presented in Mark's and Luke's accounts:

> Tell us, when shall *these things* (plural) be? and what shall be the sign when *all these things* shall be fulfilled? (Mark 13:4; see also Luke 21:7).

The wording of the disciples' questions reveals that the foremost topic of concern in their minds was the subject of Jerusalem's impending destruction; however, the way in which they closely linked their inquiries about the sign of His coming and the end of the world strongly suggests that they were ignorantly assuming that these events would be contemporaneous—as Alfred Edersheim noted,

> . . . the language of the synoptics seems to indicate that they had not clearly understood the words of the Lord which they reported, and that in their own minds they had associated the "last signs" and the advent of Christ with the fall of the city. Thus may they have come to expect that blessed advent even in their own days.[1]

By observing the manner in which they framed their inquiry, we may safely conclude that the disciples had erroneously taken for granted that when the alien armies began to attack Jerusalem, that the Lord would return and fight against the invaders. In essence, the disciples were not separating the fulfillment of these events (i.e., Jerusalem's destruction, His visible return, and the end of the age) by an indeterminate space of time; instead, they were presenting to Jesus, in the form of several questions, what to them were a series of interlocking events scheduled to transpire within their generation. In the confused apocalyptic thinking of the

---

1. Alfred Edersheim, *The Life and Times of Jesus the Messiah*, p. 450.

disciples, they were lumping together both the destruction of Jerusalem, and the consummation of the age. Christ's earlier revelations concerning Jerusalem's impending judgment had produced a deep sense of perplexity in the disciples, "who were inclined to believe that the temple was as permanent as the world itself and therefore felt that the destruction of the temple would mark the end of the age."[2]

This insight into the disciples' reasoning is important, because it helps explain why the Lord responded in the manner which He did. By placing these questions so closely together, the disciples were revealing how closely they associated the impending fall of Jerusalem and the second coming of Christ. Much of Christ's response is skillfully directed towards correcting this dangerous misconception lest His followers be unprepared for the coming desolation of Jerusalem.

Contrary to the widespread belief of many, the Lord did not provide, or even attempt to provide, any distinct signs which were to immediately herald His advent, except to stress that it would be totally unexpected in nature. We will examine this point in greater detail later. What He did so painstakingly strive to impress upon the disciples was that His coming would not be coincidental with Jerusalem's destruction. He carefully endeavored to establish this distinction in timing in order to protect His own following from being misled by the numerous false reports and false Christs that would be present at that time, and from looking (as thousands of Jews actually did) for a supposed miraculous deliverance. A significant portion of Christ's Olivet response is specifically geared towards protecting His people from fellowshipping this delusion. The Lord purposely endeavored to correct the disciples' misconceptions concerning any linkage of

---

2. George Murray, *Millennial Studies*, p. 7.

Jerusalem's destruction with His return. He informed His disciples of the fact that the timing of His return was in no way connected with the events which He was so carefully forewarning them of. His primary objective was not to provide those disciples with definite signs of His second coming, but to alert that very generation of believers of the approaching holocaust awaiting Jerusalem. Only after providing His followers with adequate information concerning that catastrophic event, the specific sign preceding it, and the necessary instructions to insure their safe evacuation from the doomed city and surrounding countryside did He begin to address the secondary and less-pressing issue of His second coming and the end of the world.

The Primary Thrust of the Olivet Prophecy

It is absolutely imperative that those who seek an accurate interpretation of the Olivet prophecy must, first and foremost, recognize that the principle thrust of Christ's prophetic response centered upon the subject of Jerusalem's impending destruction and then secondarily upon the far less urgent issue of the end of the world. Each of the gospel accounts record the primary question which the disciples had raised in response to Christ's disturbing revelation about Jerusalem's destruction:

MATT. 24	MARK 13	LUKE 21
3 And as he sat upon the mount of Olives, the disciples came unto him privately, saying, Tell us, when shall these things be? and what *shall be* the sign of thy coming, and of the end of the world?	3 And as he sat upon the mount of Olives over against the temple, Peter and James and John and Andrew asked him privately, 4 Tell us, when shall these things be? and what *shall be* the sign when all these things shall be fulfilled?	7 And they asked him, saying, Master, but when shall these things be? and what sign *will there be* when these things shall come to pass?

10

Each version records this essential issue of concern to the disciples. However, in addition to the fundamental question of the timing of the temple's destruction, Matthew's account includes the disciples' additional questions involving the end of the age which they had presumptuously and erroneously linked to the main topic of Jerusalem's destruction:

What shall be the sign of thy coming, and of the end of the world?

Many approach a study of the Olivet discourse with the mistaken assumption that the only question the disciples asked concerned the sign of Christ's coming and the end of the world, and that the entire focus of Christ's response centered upon the final events at the end of the age. For example, Charles Ryrie claims that, "In this discourse Jesus answers two of the three questions the disciples asked. . . . He does not answer 'When shall these things be?' [that is, the issue of Jerusalem's coming desolation] . . . He answers 'What will be the sign of your coming?'"[3] The error of failing to recognize the fact that two essential questions were raised and that the primary question presented involved the impending destruction of Jerusalem, has worked to establish a distorted framework of interpretation which adversely affects major portions of this prophecy, and indirectly contributes to a misinterpretation of many other prophetic passages.

Numerous scholars have overlooked the immense weight of significance which Jesus attached to the destruction of Jerusalem in 70 A.D., to the termination of Jewish national existence, and to the resulting worldwide dispersion of the

---

3. Charles C. Ryrie, *The Ryrie Study Bible*, p. 1489.

survivors of the Roman holocaust. "They forget that the destruction of Jerusalem and the excision of the Jewish nation from the kingdom was one of the most important events that has ever occurred on earth, and had tremendous consequences for the future of earth."[4] It is a pity that many have fallen short from comprehending the prominent role which these events played in the divine chronology and in the prophetic witness of the Old Testament (i.e., "The times of Jacob's trouble," Jeremiah 30:7; "a time of trouble such as never was since there was a nation," Daniel 12:1). This simple but tragic oversight has contributed to hindering the sound interpretation of this important prophetic discourse.

Untold confusion has been the direct result of failing to recognize that major scriptural sections in the Olivet response have already witnessed their unmistakable historic fulfillments. The failure to accept this fact has resulted in leaving the Christian community with a confusing and often contradictory jumble of unfulfilled predictions and prophetic loose ends for which the prophetic student is forced to concoct some fanciful future application in time. This error has produced two essentially harmful results:

1. We are thus deprived of the evidential value, and the support to the faith, of those remarkable fulfillments of prophecy which are so clearly presented to us as authentic contemporary histories; and,
2. Our vision of things to come is greatly obscured by the transference to the future of predicted events which, in fact, have already happened, and whereof complete records have been preserved for our information.[5]

---

4. J. Marcellus Kik, *Matthew Twenty-Four*, p. 21.
5. Philip Mauro, *Seventy Weeks and the Great Tribulation*, p. 194.

Before successfully embarking upon any balanced study of unfulfilled prophecy, it is absolutely essential that we first determine those prophetic facts which have already found their fulfillment in great historical events of the past. Obviously, we cannot possibly succeed in any successful study of unfulfilled prophecy until we have settled our minds as to the predicted things which have already come to pass. The failure to do this has resulted in transferring the bulk of Jesus' prophetic statements to an unfulfilled, futuristic context. The tragedy of this error is that it creates a highly speculative scenario of end-time events which is misleading to the people of God, and works to obscure a balanced scriptural perspective of, and a response to, the demands and challenges of the last days.

The landscape of prophetic interpretation has been cluttered with the verbal litter of dispensationalism in recent years. This dispensationalist school of prophetic interpretation refuses to accept the blatant reality that significant portions of Jesus' Olivet discourse were directly related to the destruction of Jerusalem in 70 A.D. I take issue with this common tendency and join the ranks of those who have pointed out that when Christ warned His disciples of the "great tribulation" (Matthew 24:21), "the days of vengeance" (Luke 21:22), and the "days of affliction" (Mark 13:19) that were to come, He was referring to the approaching calamities attending the destruction of Jerusalem in 70 A.D., and not to a highly speculative, end-time tribulation preceding the second coming.

It is essential to realize that Jesus was devoting much of His comments to answering the fundamental question posed by His disciples which focused primarily upon the issue of Jerusalem's impending destruction. The Lord's own predictions and warnings concerning this event, which was then

13

close at hand, were most explicit, and He plainly stated that, *all these things shall come upon this generation* (Matthew 23:36; see also 24:34). In addressing this principal issue, Jesus provided substantial detail and explicit warnings concerning the signs preceding this event and its precise timing. I believe that the statements of Jesus concerning the holocaust of 70 A.D. are absolutely clear and the context of His comments most transparent.

One of the principle aims of this book is to establish precisely this and to present with all possible care the available proofs from scripture and reliable secular history whereby we can firmly establish that the *great tribulation* of Matthew 24:21 is not a future event but an established fact of past history, and that many sections of this prophecy which have been erroneously applied to the end times have long ago found their fulfillments. Furthermore, though I accept the fact that Jesus did, indeed, devote attention to addressing the secondary questions involving the sign of His coming and the end of the world, He did so in a brief manner and without directing the bulk of His prophetic response to elaborating upon these inquiries. I believe that a careful examination of the Olivet discourse in relation to these points will aid us immeasurably in comprehending this, as well as many other related prophetic passages. In the following chapters, I will present a comprehensive exposition of the Olivet prophecies in parallel, in an attempt to establish a balanced, scriptural perspective on each of the essential questions raised by the disciples and, in so doing, help equip Christians with the necessary insights and understanding needed to victoriously face the actual conditions and tests of the last days.

Questions for Discussion

1. Why is context so crucial to an accurate interpretation of the Mount Olivet discourse? Does the chapter break between Matthew chapter 23 and 24 tend to break the natural sequence of thought and obscure context?
2. Is it justifiable to label the Mount Olivet discourse the "pivotal prophecy of scripture"? Why?
3. Do you believe Christ's prophetic appraisal of the church age should hold a preeminent position of importance above other prophecies? Why?
4. Do you agree with the "domino principle" in respect to the Olivet prophecy's relationship and impact upon other prophetic passages? Please explain.
5. In sound biblical interpretation, the obscure or enigmatic passage must always yield to the clear. Do you feel that some current prophetic systems are built more upon the obscure, or the clear statements of scripture? Have Christ's prophetic statements often been forced to yield to the more obscure passages of prophecy?
6. Why has this principle of interpretation been so commonly ignored in the realm of prophetic interpretation?
7. Do you feel that a disproportionate emphasis has been placed upon such enigmatic prophecies as the Book of Revelation when developing prophetic perspectives?
8. Discuss how a rigid prophetic system or prejudice can negatively influence a balanced interpretation of prophecy. Can you give an outstanding example where an interpreter's prophetic bias has done an injustice to the obvious meaning of a prophetic passage?
9. Discuss the detrimental results of holding a futuristic outlook toward prophecy which has already been fulfilled.

10. Does the fact that Christ had to carefully correct the disciple's prophetic misconceptions suggest the possibility that our prophetic assumptions may also be in error? Are we any less prone to misconceptions than they? What cautions should this instill in us when approaching prophecy?

THE WARNING OF FALSE CHRISTS

Chapter One

THE WARNING OF FALSE CHRISTS

MATT. 24	MARK 13	LUKE 21
4 And Jesus answered and said unto them, Take heed that no man deceive you.	5 And Jesus answering them began to say, Take heed lest any *man* deceive you:	8 And he said, Take heed that ye be not deceived: for many shall come in my name, saying, I am *Christ* and the time draweth near: go ye not therefore after them.
5 For many shall come in my name, saying, I am Christ; and shall deceive many.	6 For many shall come in my name, saying, I am *Christ*; and shall deceive many.	

Wars, devastating quakes, the spread of disease, and famine—these were the first glimpses of the sorrows which lay ahead. As the Lord launched into His initial appraisal of the church age, His words carried little assurances of future tranquility. Instead, He paints a grim picture of coming distress, destruction, and upheaval. For the disciples poised on the threshold of this age, Christ's prophetic scenario was indeed sobering.

The Initial Warning

The opening thrust of Christ's Olivet response centers upon the first in a series of warnings concerning the general signs which would precede the destruction of Jerusalem. His disciples had asked for a sign which would signalize the timing of Jerusalem's destruction and its temple; but before revealing the specific sign, He commences His discourse by mentioning certain misleading signs which might cause them to assume that the end of Jerusalem was immediately at hand.

His primary focus was upon the imminent upheavals which were to befall the historic time frame of 35-70 A.D. However, in a secondary and much broader context, the signs which He lists represent a sweeping characterization

18

of the general disturbances which would so accurately typify the entire breadth of this age. The Lord was carefully cautioning His disciples with the sobering reality that certain distresses would transpire before Jerusalem's destruction, and by so doing, was endeavoring to protect them from prematurely concluding that each new outbreak of turmoil was the definite sign that Israel's predicted ruin was near. In a far broader sense, the Lord was equally striving to caution His followers of every generation from prematurely assuming that every new crisis or natural disorder was the infallible proof that the end was near.

Pseudo-Christs

The initial warning involves the subject of spiritual deceivers who would arise in His absence, declaring that they were the Christ (or Messiah) and would deceive many. Though the emergence of false prophets and counterfeit Christs has been a repeated occurrence throughout the church age, these warnings were specifically directed toward those disciples, and were intended to warn them of the impending danger that was drawing near. Luke's record adds the explicit statement that ". . . THE TIME DRAWETH NEAR: go ye not therefore after them."

His disciples were to remain cautious and alert lest they fall prey to the deceptive claims and false assurances which these spiritual imposters would proclaim. Many would arise during that generation with fabricated revelations that the Lord's return was at hand (see Matthew 24:23-26). It is an historical fact, as we shall see, that numerous messianic pretenders rose up at the time of Jerusalem's siege and deceived many. Not only was there a concentration of deceivers

19

during the siege of Jerusalem, but many other religious charlatans had arisen between the timing of Christ's ascension and the destruction of 70 A.D.

The Testimony of Acts

The historic chronicle of the early church recorded in the book of Acts mentions several of these predicted false Christs. In Acts, chapter 8, we read of Simon Magnus who ". . . used sorcery, and bewitched the people of Samaria giving out that himself was some great one: to whom they all gave heed . . . saying, This man is the great power of God" (Acts 8:9, 10). Jerome quotes him as claiming, "I am the word of God, I am the comforter, I am almighty, I am all there is of God."[1] In Acts, chapter 5, we read of Theudas, a false prophet who ". . . rose up . . . in the days of the taxing, and drew away much people after him" (Acts 5:37). In Acts, chapter 13, we read of Paul's confrontation with the Jewish false prophet named Bar-Jesus.

Secular history also records the presence of false Christs and deceivers, and works to corroborate the predictions of Jesus. The Jewish historian Josephus stated that many pretenders arose claiming divine inspiration. They deceived multitudes by leading them into the desert declaring that God would show them miraculous signs of deliverance from the Roman powers.[2] He also referred to the Egyptian false prophet, Theudas, mentioned in Acts 5:36, who deceived many with his claims of divine assistance. Origen mentions another deceiver named Dositheus who asserted that he

---

1. Henry L. Mansel, *The Gnostic Heresies of the 1st and 2nd Centuries*, p. 82.
2. Flavius Josephus, *Wars*, Bk. 2, Chp. 13.

was the Christ foretold by Moses. Jerome mentions a deceiver by the name of Barchochebas who claimed to vomit flames. Josephus even noted that during the reign of Nero, while Felix was procurator of Judea (Acts 23:26), deceivers and false prophets were so rampant that some were apprehended and executed almost on a daily basis.[3]

Questions for Discussion

1. In referring to the general signs which would characterize this age, why did Jesus mention the sign of false Christs first?
2. Why is there a greater danger of being deceived by false Christs during times of instability and turmoil?
3. Can you name any false Christs which have arisen during the church age? What would be some prominent examples of people being deceived by false Messiahs within the last 150 years?
4. Discuss some common characteristics which seem to typify false Christs.
5. Does the fact that Christ had to specifically warn Christians not to follow after false Christs say anything about their deceptive power?

---

3. Flavius Josephus, *Antiquities*, Bk. 20, Chps. 4 and 7.

"WARS AND RUMORS OF WARS"

Chapter Two

"WARS AND RUMORS OF WARS"

MATT. 24	MARK 13	LUKE 21
6 And ye shall hear of wars and rumours of wars; see that ye be not troubled: for all *these things* must come to pass, but the end is not yet.	7 And when ye shall hear of wars and rumours of wars, be ye not troubled: for *such things* must needs be; but the end *shall* not *be* yet.	9 But when ye shall hear of wars and commotions, be not terrified: for these things must first come to pass; but the end *is* not by and by.
7 For nation shall rise against nation, and kingdom dom against kingdom:	8 For nation shall rise against nation, and kingdom dom against kingdom:	10 Then said he unto them, Nation shall rise against nation, and kingdom against kingdom.

Though the terrors of war loomed on the horizon, the disciples were cautioned not to be frightened by their outbreak or the rumors preceding them. These were important instructions for the disciples and were given to protect them from the danger of overreacting in the face of troublesome times. The wisdom of this simple exhortation has been needed by *every* generation of believers.

Troublesome Times

At the timing of this prophecy, the Empire was enjoying a relative degree of peace (*Pax Romana*) within its borders, but within a short time the Empire found itself convulsing under the repeated blows of civil disorders, insurrections, and wars within its territory as well as upon its frontiers. The noted Roman historian, Tacitus, recorded the turmoil of the times in the "Annuls of Tacitus" which covered the period of Roman history prior to 70 A.D. In this work, the descriptive expressions of civil strife are frequently mentioned: "The war in Britain," "war in Armenia," "disturbances in Germany," "insurrections in Gaul," "intrigues among the Parthians," "commotions in Africa," and "commotions in Thrace."

23

The forty year period between the Olivet prophecy and Jerusalem's destruction witnessed an ever-increasing number of civil disturbances involving the Jews. An uprising in Caesarea cost the lives of 20,000 Jews; at Scythopolis, 13,000 Jews were slaughtered; in Alexandria, an uprising cost the Jews 50,000 slain; another 10,000 Jews were killed in Damascus. Josephus recorded the turbulence of the times, especially in regards to the *rumors of wars*, when Emperor Caligula ordered his statue to be erected in the temple at Jerusalem (40 A.D.). The Jews refused to obey the Roman dictate and lived in a state of constant expectation of imminent war with the Romans, and were in such consternation on the occasion that they even neglected to till the land.[1]

The turbulence of that period can be reflected in the deaths of four successive emperors ("the year of the four emperors") who experienced violent ends within an 18 month period (68-69 A.D.) prior to Jerusalem's destruction. With such violence attending the reigns of these emperors prior to the fall of Jerusalem, it is little wonder that the Empire experienced increasing distress, insecurity, and restlessness.

Not a Sign of the End

In spite of the violence which was predicted to increasingly characterize the period prior to Jerusalem's destruction, the disciples were explicitly warned that this state of growing unrest was not to be taken as an obvious indication of the end. Though wars would break out, and they would increasingly hear the rumors of wars, the disciples were cautioned

---

1. Flavius Josephus, *Antiquities*, Bk. 18, Chp. 9, and *Wars*, Bk. 2, Chp. 10.

not to be troubled. Jesus specified that these distresses would have to come to pass. They were not the sign of the end: ". . . BUT THE END IS NOT YET" (Matthew 24:6b). It is my conviction that the *end* to which Jesus refers has an immediate reference to the termination of the Jewish polity in 70 A.D., and then only in a secondary sense, to the end of the world.

These commotions were to be the general features of the period prior to Jerusalem's destruction in particular, as well as the church age in general. They were not to be taken as the specific sign of either Jerusalem's destruction, or the end of the world. They were given to show that "the *end* is not yet" (Matthew 24:6b; Mark 13:7b; Luke 21:9b). The apostles were to be prepared for the emergence of wars and rumors of wars, but were not to view them as the re-quested sign immediately preceding either event. This warning served to guard the disciples from fear, confusion, and the danger of foolishly reacting in the face of violent disturbances in the world. Furthermore, it cautioned the disciples from expecting Jerusalem's ruin too early, and prepared them for the sobering reality that they would have to pass through troublesome times before Jerusalem's end arrived, and in a far broader sense, before the end of the world. When the set time arrived, a specific sign would be provided, but in the interim, they could expect to increas-ingly hear of wars and rumors of wars.

Wars and rumors of wars were to be one of the character-istic features of this age, and we are admonished not to view them at any time as decisive proofs of the end, whether Jerusalem's end, or the end of this age. "Obviously that warning applies throughout the entire age; for if commotions of the sort mentioned by the Lord were not indications of the nearness of His coming at the beginning of the age, they would not be indications thereof at any later period!"[2] In fact, wars and rumors of wars ". . . are neither the sign that the end of the age is near, nor that the end of the age is distant."[3]

This simple warning has been needed throughout the church age in order to guard God's people from the presumption of date setting, and the folly accompanying it. However, even in the face of such an explicit caution, it is surprising that Christians have persistently disregarded it and have tended to do just the opposite. Jesus was well aware that His disciples would be prone to view the periodic outbreak of wars and rumors of wars as clear indications of both the destruction of Jerusalem, as well as the end of the world. Therefore, He wisely inserted the caution that the sign of wars and rumors of wars were not to be taken as decisive proofs of the end, and added, "these things must come to pass" before the end.

Questions for Discussion

1. Explain why wars, historically, have been pointed to more than any other sign as an obvious indication of the end.
2. Why do hostilities in the Mideast seem to intensify this tendency?
3. In spite of Christ's firm warning that wars and rumors of wars were not to be viewed as a sign of the end, why have so many Christians ignored this caution and done exactly the opposite? Can you provide an example where you have personally violated this warning?

2. Philip Mauro, *Seventy Weeks and the Great Tribulation*, p. 222.
3. G. Campbell Morgan, *Gospel According to Mark*, p. 278.

4. Why have Christians tended to give more attention to prophetic speculation and sensationalism than to Christ's prophetic cautions?
5. How would the current concern over nuclear prolifica-tion and the escalating arms race relate to Christ's warn-ing about "rumors of wars"? Discuss why His warning is especially relevant to the church today, in light of the present state of global tension and potential for armed conflict.
6. Can you mention any classic examples where wars or rumors of wars have been viewed as a sign of the end?
7. As a project, list some pertinent quotes from contempo-rary prophetic literature which point to wars and rumors of wars as an indication of the nearness of the end. In light of Christ's cautions against this, are we safe in ignor-ing His warning today?
8. Why wouldn't another major war or military conflict in the Mideast necessarily be a definite sign of the end according to Christ's warning in Matthew 24:6?

FAMINES, PESTILENCES, AND EARTHQUAKES

Chapter Three

FAMINES, PESTILENCES, AND EARTHQUAKES

MATT. 24	MARK 13	LUKE 21
7 For nation shall rise against nation, and kingdom against kingdom: and there shall be famines, and pestilences, and earthquakes, in divers places.	8 For nation shall rise against nation, and kingdom against kingdom: and there shall be earthquakes in divers places, and there shall be famines and troubles: these *are* the beginnings of sorrows.	11 And great earthquakes shall be in divers places, and famines, and pestilences; and fearful sights and great signs shall there be from heaven.

Famines, disease, earthquakes, and fearful signs from heaven were rapidly approaching. In continuing His series of warnings involving the general signs which would emerge prior to Jerusalem's destruction, Christ now focuses upon certain natural calamities and fearful sights which would first appear. Though this age has repeatedly witnessed the outbreak of these natural disorders, it must be noted that Jesus' warnings concerning their occurrence were specifically directed towards His contemporaries prior to the holocaust of 70 A.D.

The Signs of Famines and Pestilences

These have been grouped together because they commonly occur in conjunction. Insufficient food or improper provisions inevitably lead to the spread of disease. The book of Acts records the outbreak of famine early in the history of the New Testament church. In Acts 11:28, the prophet Agabus foretold of a grievous famine "throughout all the world . . . in the days of Claudius Caesar" (44 A.D.). The direct impact upon Judea was reflected by the fact that the disciples at Antioch mounted an urgent relief mission in order to ease the burden afflicting the Judean Christians

29

(Acts 11:29). Josephus noted that this famine was so severe at Jerusalem that many perished from lack of food.[1]

Besides the famine in Judea, three other famines appeared during the reign of Claudius: one in Greece, mentioned by Eusebius, and two in Rome, the first mentioned by Dio Cassius, the second by Tacitus. The Roman historian, Suetonius also recorded famines during that period. Tacitus mentioned a "failure in the crops, and a famine consequent thereupon."

The spread of disease was also present in these days. Suetonius mentions "pestilence" in Rome during the reign of Nero which was so severe that "within the space of one autumn there died no less than 30,000 persons." Josephus stated that plagues raged in Babylonia in 40 A.D. Tacitus speaks of epidemics in Italy in 66 A.D.

The Sign of Earthquakes

Jesus stated that there would be earthquakes in many places. The New Testament documents several. We read of a great earthquake in conjunction with Christ's crucifixion (Matthew 27:51-54); another is mentioned at Christ's resurrection (Matthew 28:2). In Acts 16:26, we read of a great earthquake striking the colony city of Philippi. Devastating quakes occurred during the reigns of Caligula and Claudius. In Claudius' reign, earthquakes happened in Crete, Smyrna, Miletus, Chios, and Samos. Tacitus mentioned earthquakes at Rome. He recorded that, "Frequent earthquakes occurred, by which many houses were thrown down," and that "twelve populous cities of Asia fell in ruins

---

1. Flavius Josephus, *Antiquities*, Bk. 20, Chp. 2:5.

from an earthquake." A quake occurred in 54 A.D. on the day Nero assumed the toga. Another quake was mentioned to have occurred in 60 A.D. during the reign of Nero in the city of Laodicea in which the city was devastated along with the neighboring cities of Hierapolis and Colossae. Seneca wrote in 58 A.D.,

> How often have the cities of Asia and Achaea fallen with one fatal shock! How many cities have been swallowed up in Syria! How many in Macedonia! How often has Paphos become a ruin! News has often been brought to us of the demolition of whole cities at once.

Seneca also mentioned one in Campania; Suetonius mentioned one in Rome during the reign of Galba (68 A.D.). The city of Pompeii was destroyed in 63 A.D. by an earthquake. Josephus recorded a major earthquake in Judea which was accompanied by violent winds, vehement showers, continual lightnings, and terrible thunderings. He further commented: "These things were a manifest indication that some destruction was coming upon men . . . and anyone would guess that these wonders foreshadowed some grand calamities that were coming."[2]

Signs from Heaven

Only Luke's account records this sign. Though many would tend to place this sign at the end of the age due to its supernatural quality, the context of Luke's account places this phenomenon prior to the siege of Jerusalem in 70 A.D. By "great signs from heaven," Jesus was probably referring to catastrophic upheavals in nature such as meteor showers, devastating storms, volcanic eruptions, and cyclones which would strike terror in the hearts of men.

---

2. Flavius Josephus, *Wars*, Bk. 4, Chp. 4:5.

Josephus refers to several of these *fearful sights* occurring prior to Jerusalem's destruction:

a) He mentions a star which hung over the city like a sword; and a comet which lasted a whole year; b) during the night of the feast of unleavened bread, a "great light" shone about the altar and the temple which continued for half an hour; c) the eastern gate of the temple which was constructed of solid brass and was very heavy and could barely be shut by twenty men, was observed to "open of its own accord about the sixth hour"; d) all over the country, chariots and armies fighting in the clouds and besieging cities was witnessed. The Roman historian Tacitus corroborated this sign by adding that, "Continuing hosts were seen meeting in the skies, arms flashed, and suddenly the temple was illuminated with fire from the clouds. Of a sudden the doors of the shrine opened and a superhuman voice cried: 'The gods are departing'; at the same moment the mighty stir of their going was heard."; e) four years prior to Jerusalem's siege, Jesus the son of Ananus came to the feast of tabernacles and ran up and down the streets day and night crying: "A voice from the east! A voice from the west! A voice from the four winds! A voice against Jerusalem and the temple! A voice against the bridegrooms and the brides! A voice against all the people!" Though he was scourged and tortured by the officials in order to silence him, he could not be restrained. He continued raving for seven years, "Woe, woe to the city and to the people and to the temple!" His lamentation continued every day until he was finally killed during Jerusalem's siege shouting, "Woe, woe to myself also!"[3]

---

3. *Ibid.*, Bk. 6, Chp. 5:3, 4.

No doubt, some of these sensationalized reports were the product of rumor and cannot be verified as fact or fiction. Though they must be treated with a measure of skepticism, the very fact that Josephus records them demonstrates that they were being widely circulated prior to Jerusalem's destruction. This fact lends support to the intended purpose of Christ's warning. It was precisely because of such rumored signs that He so painstakingly cautioned His followers. They were not to be terrified by such reports. They were not to foolishly overreact, or prematurely assume that these signs signaled Jerusalem's imminent destruction.

Questions for Discussion

1. As a project, research the subject of earthquakes and try to determine whether dispensationalist claims of a steadily increasing frequency of quakes is accurate.
2. Can you list any major earthquakes, famines, or plagues during church history which have caused their contemporaries to assume the end was imminent?
3. Why does the outbreak of famines, pestilences, and earthquakes affecting the natural order of creation tend to foster an alarm that the end may be near?
4. Discuss what you feel Jesus meant by "fearful sights and great signs" from heaven. Was He referring to natural or spiritual phenomena? Please explain your reasons.
5. Would the current interest in the "Jupiter effect," Halley's Comet, U.F.O.'s, or space exploration have any bearing on Christ's mention of "fearful sights and great signs" from heaven?
6. Is there any justification in relating Josephus' mention of the unusual phenomena prior to 70 A.D. to Christ's mention of "fearful sights and great signs" from heaven?

"THE BEGINNING OF SORROWS"

34

Chapter Four

"THE BEGINNING OF SORROWS"

MATT. 24	MARK 13	LUKE 21
8 All these *are* the beginning of sorrows.	8 For nation shall rise against nation, and kingdom against kingdom: and there shall be earthquakes in divers places, and there shall be famines and troubles: these *are* the beginnings of sorrows.	

Were these the catastrophic signs of the end? Were they the terrors reserved for the final countdown before the end of the world? Was Christ revealing the last awesome woes to be unleashed upon humanity at the close of this age, or were they simply the general *signs of the times* characterizing the entire breadth of this turbulent age?

Only General Woes

In outlining the general upheavals which would soon arise, the Lord cautioned that they should be viewed as only the *beginning of sorrows.* The clash of nations and the outbreak of famines, pestilence and earthquakes were inevitable, but the disciples were warned not to ignorantly assume that these signs marked the eve of His return or that they were the sign of Jerusalem's impending destruction. None of these distresses were meant to herald the end. In fact, Jesus reveals that they were simply the initial birth throes of a new dispensation. None of these general *sorrows* were meant, at any time, to mislead Christians into the erroneous assumption that either His advent was imminent, or that God's judgments were about to befall Jerusalem. On this point Edersheim wisely noted:

35

And, as regards the more general cosmic signs (Matthew 24:6-8), have not Christians in the early ages watched, not only the wars on the boundaries of the Empire, but the condition of the state in the age of Nero, the risings, turmoils, and threatenings; and so onwards, those of later generations, even down to the commotions of our own period, as if they betokened the immediate Advent of Christ, instead of marking in them only the beginning of the birth-throes of the new "Age"?[1]

The World in Travail

The phrase, "the beginning of sorrows," is only recorded in Matthew's and Mark's accounts and calls for special attention. The word "sorrow" is translated from the Greek word *ōdin* meaning "birth pangs, travail, and pain." It was used metaphorically to compare the sufferings and distress that would characterize the church age to the suffering of a woman travailing in the process of birth. This word depicts the present age as one of pains and sorrows such as accompany childbirth. But even though this age is characterized by suffering, there is a distinctly hopeful nature to such afflictions, for they will eventually culminate in the joy of delivery. This age is a period of birth pangs preceding the birth of a new era.

In Romans 8:22, the same word occurs in verb form (*sunōdinō*):

For we know that the whole creation groaneth and *travaileth* in pain together until now.

---

1. Alfred Edersheim, *The Life and Times of Jesus the Messiah*, p. 447.

The groaning which Paul speaks of is in reference to the entire creation's earnest expectation *for the manifestation of the sons of God* (Romans 8:19). In the same context, Paul speaks of the joyful outcome of such suffering:

> And not only they (creation), but ourselves also . . . groan within ourselves, waiting for the adoption, to wit, the redemption of our body (Romans 8:23).

The "adoption" which Paul speaks of is the "manifestation of the sons of God." We are also told that the creation itself also "shall be delivered from the bondage of corruption into the glorious liberty of the children of God" (Romans 8:21) at that time. In the light of these perspectives, we can view the sorrows of the church age against the backdrop of creation's travail as she expectantly awaits the birth of a new age at Christ's coming.

The word *travail (ōdin)* is found in a similar connection in I Thessalonians 5:3 where, in speaking of the second coming of Christ, Paul states:

> For when they shall say, Peace and safety; then sudden destruction cometh upon them, as *travail upon a woman* with child; and they shall not escape.

In comparing Christ's statement concerning "the beginning of sorrows" with Paul's comments concerning the travail which will accompany the end of the world, we can conclude that the distresses and pains that began early in the church's history will visit the earth with an intensified force at the end of this age in immediate conjunction with the return of Christ in judgment.

It is helpful to note that after the initial, intense pains accompanying actual childbirth, the pains are intermittent in nature until the very end when they increase in intensity and are the most severe of all. Likewise, this dispensation, which commenced with the *beginning of sorrows,* has historically experienced intermittent birth pangs (wars, famines, pestilences, and earthquakes) throughout its course and will climax with the final, intense travail of *sudden destruction* at the consummation of the age.

It must be noted that though there may be a noticeable emergence of sorrows accompanying the closing hours of this dispensation, the frequency of such occurrences throughout the entire church age prevents them from serving as precursory signs of the Lord's impending advent. As we will see, the Lord's statements were absolutely emphatic on this crucial point. However, in spite of this fact, Christians have historically tended to regard every major international conflict, crisis, threat of war, or natural calamity as an undeniable proof of the end. This error has historically resulted in multitudes of Christians being misled by foolish speculations which have negatively impacted upon their mental, spiritual, and physical attitude and response. We will examine this issue in greater detail in the course of this study.

Questions for Discussion

1. Is it justifiable to characterize the church age as one of suffering and travail? What about from a secular perspective?
2. Is the Christian view of history pessimistic, optimistic, or both? Should it be pessimistic? Please explain.
3. Do you agree with the statement that the frequency of wars, famines, pestilences, and earthquakes prevents

them from serving as a precursory sign of the second coming? Please elaborate.

4. Does the phrase, "all these things are the beginning of sorrows" imply that wars, rumors of wars, and natural disorders are simply the general "signs of the times" characterizing this entire age? Has history proven this to be the case? In light of this statement, should the church expect these general signs to cease during this age? Using scripture, discuss what the church's reaction should be to the emergence of these signs. How should our response differ from that of unbelievers?

5. In the context of mentioning wars and rumors of wars, Mark's account adds: "for such things must needs be" (Mark 13:7). Why are these things necessary?

6. Besides the general signs referred to by Christ, can you list any other signs which are commonly pointed to as indications of the end?

PERSECUTION AND FALSE PROPHETS

Chapter Five

PERSECUTION AND FALSE PROPHETS

MATT. 24	MARK 13	LUKE 21
9 Then shall they deliver you up to be afflicted, and shall kill you: and ye shall be hated of all nations for my name's sake. 10 And then shall many be offended, and shall betray one another, and shall hate one another. 11 And many false prophets shall rise, and shall deceive many. 12 And because iniquity shall abound, the love of many shall wax cold. 13 But he that shall endure unto the end, the same shall be saved. 14 And this gospel of the kingdom shall be preached in all the world for a witness unto all nations; and then shall the end come.	9 But take heed to yourselves: for they shall deliver you up to councils; and in the synagogues ye shall be beaten: and ye shall be brought before rulers and kings for my sake, for a testimony against them. 10 And the gospel must first be published among all nations. 11 But when they shall lead you, and deliver you up, take no thought beforehand what ye shall speak, neither do ye premeditate; but whatsoever shall be given you in that hour, that speak ye: for it is not ye that speak, but the Holy Ghost. 12 Now the brother shall betray the brother to death, and the father the son; and children shall rise up against *their* parents; and shall cause them to be put to death. 13 And ye shall be hated of all *men* for my name's sake: but he that shall endure unto the end, the same shall be saved.	12 But before all these, they shall lay their hands on you, and persecute *you*, delivering *you* up to the synagogues, and into prisons, being brought before kings and rulers for my name's sake. 13 And it shall turn to you for a testimony. 14 Settle *it* therefore in your hearts, not to meditate before what ye shall answer: 15 For I will give you a mouth and wisdom, which all your adversaries shall not be able to gainsay nor resist. 16 And ye shall be betrayed both by parents, and brethren, and kinsfolks, and friends; and *some* of you shall they cause to be put to death. 17 And ye shall be hated of all *men* for my name's sake. 18 But there shall not an hair of your head perish. 19 In your patience possess ye your souls.

Christ's grim predictions of coming turmoil now pass from the general sphere affecting the world to the particular sphere of the church. He does so by indicating the two general perils which would potentially jeopardize the faith of the believers—the external danger of persecution, and the internal threat of false prophets who would arise and deceive many. Each would have a destructive impact upon the church.

41

The Rise of Persecution

Jesus now cautions the disciples from being misled by the presumptuous notion that the gospel would divinely shelter them from the inevitable persecutions they would endure. Though they were destined to weather opposition, hostilities, and betrayal, they were given the consoling assurance that divine assistance would be imparted in the hour of need to effectively enable them to testify before kings, rulers, and Jewish tribunals. He was encouraging them that the very persecutions which they would face would be redeemed as a vehicle to present the gospel of Christ.

The coming persecutions would not be isolated only to the early church, but would be one of the characteristic plights of the entire church age. Some persecutions have been limited in nature and generated from local discontent and opposition to the gospel (see Acts 13:50, 51; 14:18, 19; 16:19-23; 17:5-10; 19:23-41), while others were sanctioned under the auspices of the civil or ecclesiastical authorities (see Acts 7:54-60; 8:1; 9:1, 2; Acts 23; the Neronian persecution 64-68 A.D.). Some have been minor in scale and limited to verbal abuse and ostracism, while others have been severe and far-reaching resulting in torture, imprisonment, banishment, confiscation of properties, and martyrdom.

Though every generation of believers has faced the threat of persecution, these specific warnings had an immediate bearing upon the disciples of *that* generation, poised on the brink of Jerusalem's destruction. The wording of Mark's account calls for close attention:

> But take heed to yourselves: for they shall deliver you up to councils and in the synagogues ye shall be beaten (Mark 13:9; see also Luke 21:12).

The reference to synagogues and councils limits the timing of this warning to the period prior to 70 A.D. The word *councils* is translated from the Greek word *sunedria* and is the same word used for the "Sanhedrin" in Jerusalem. This was the ruling ecclesiastical body of the Jewish nation which repeatedly opposed the early church. The synagogues represented the Jewish religious and civil authorities on a local level. It must be pointed out that with the destruction of Jerusalem in 70 A.D., the entire Jewish polity collapsed. What power the Jewish rulers were able to wield against the Christians prior to 70 A.D. was effectively terminated after that date. With this fact in mind, we see that the primary thrust of these statements was specifically directed towards the early Christians prior to Jerusalem's destruction. Christ was bracing the disciples of that generation for the opposition they would face before the destruction of Jerusalem.

The book of Acts records a variety of persecutions inflicted upon the early believers during the historical period prior to 70 A.D. (Acts 4, 5, 6, 8, 13, 14, 18, 21, 22, 24, 25). However, in keeping with Jesus' Olivet assurances that "it shall turn to you for a testimony" (Luke 21:13), they were given wisdom to effectively testify before their accusers.

Looking beyond the historical chronicle of Acts, we discover that Christ's predictions of persecution were even more aptly fulfilled during the Neronian persecution (64-68 A.D.). Thousands of Christians were butchered in the most fiendish and diabolical manner. During this wave of persecution, Peter and Paul laid down their lives for the gospel, but not before Paul was able to make "the preaching . . . fully known . . . that all the Gentiles might hear" (II Timothy 4:17) in the very courts of the Emperor himself.

In light of this capsulized overview of the early church's persecution, we see that the Olivet predictions were literally fulfilled. Christians were dragged before synagogues, the Sanhedrin, and Roman rulers. They were afflicted, beaten, betrayed, imprisoned, and killed. Yet, in spite of the severity of their treatment, they repeatedly redeemed their situations to powerfully testify of the truth of the gospel of Jesus Christ (see Acts 4:5-12, 19, 20; 9:15, 16; 22:1-21; 23:1, 6, 11; 24:10-21; 26:1-29; 27:21-26; 28:23-28; II Timothy 4:17).

The Rise of False Prophets

This division of the prophecy also contains the additional warning concerning the appearance of spiritual deceivers. This warning echoes the previous cautions concerning the rise of false Christs (see Matthew 24:5; Mark 13:6; Luke 21:8). Due to the potentially devastating influence of these spiritual pretenders, the warning was repeated. Christ was informing His followers that a wide host of deceivers would appear and wreak havoc upon the church through their corruptive influence. The repeated warnings to the disciples concerning the predicted emergence of these individuals attests to the weight of significance which the Lord placed upon their dangerous influence.

Not only does the whole course of church history verify the accuracy of this prediction, but the scriptures also mention the presence of false prophets during the development of the early church or predict their eventual appearance. A number of epistles were specifically penned to counter the corrupting influence of false teachers and false doctrine (i.e., Galatians, Colossians, II Corinthians, II Timothy, II Peter, I John and Jude). Some of the epistles were written to check the influence of Judaizers (Galatians, II Corinthians), while others were written in response to the emerging development of the Gnostic philosophies (Colossians, I John,

II Peter, and Jude). With few exceptions, almost all of the New Testament letters include some warnings against the destructive impact of spiritual deceivers who would attempt to infiltrate the church. The epistles also predict the repeated appearance of these spiritual imposters and their teachings (I Timothy 4:1, 2; II Timothy 3:13; 4:3; II Peter 2:1-3).

The external threat of persecution and suffering would take its toll upon the Christian community, for He informs His followers that, "The love of many shall wax cold" (Matthew 24:12). They would witness the disheartening presence of apostasies and defections from the faith. Some would buckle under the strain of persecution and the threat of suffering, some would even betray their own loved ones and former friends, and others would desert the faith because of the seductive influence of false prophets.

A Positive Assurance

However, in spite of the growing pressures of persecution and the spread of deception and apostasy, Jesus includes positive assurances which would bolster the faith and courage of His people from sinking into hopelessness and despair:

> . . . this gospel of the kingdom must first be preached in all the world for a witness unto all nations; and then the end shall come (Matthew 24:14; see also Mark 13:10).

As has been pointed out by Edersheim and as we will enlarge upon further: "This then is the only sign [given] of 'the end' of this present age."[1] This statement encourages us that in spite of whatever opposition the church would endure, the gospel would continue its triumphant march unto the "uttermost parts of the earth." None of the chaotic conditions of

---

1. Alfred Edersheim, *The Life and Times of Jesus the Messiah*, p. 448.

the age could effectively impede the steady advance of the gospel. The disciples were not to be discouraged, disillusioned, or detoured from the proclamation of the Good News. They were to keep in mind the one supreme goal that "the gospel must first be published among all nations" (Mark 13:10) before the end would come.

The great task of evangelizing the world was not to be stalled or cut short because of an anxious expectation of the Lord's immediate return. Even the collapse of Israel would not hinder the evangelistic mission of the church. They had a great work to do, and they were solemnly entrusted with the responsibility to occupy (keep busy) until He returned (Luke 19:13). He provided this word in order to firmly establish the truth that the church's all-consuming passion was to be the Great Commission and not an end-time hysteria. The church was not to be troubled, intimidated, or carried away by the appearance of every new calamity. The end of the age would only arrive when this supreme objective had been accomplished and not before. The Lord was well aware of the tendency of all generations of believers to neglect the work of the gospel because of an imbalanced expectation and reaction towards things to come. In spite of the hardships they would have to endure as laborers for Christ, they could take consolation in the reality that they were on the winning side and their faithful perseverance in well doing would result in their inevitable deliverance at the end of the age.

They were also given the assurance that "he that endureth to the end would be saved" (Matthew 24:13; Mark 13:13). The wording of Luke's account is slightly different but contains essentially the same meaning: "In your patience possess ye [literally - 'ye shall win'] your souls" (Luke 21:19). The probable meaning is "ye shall gain the mastery over your souls, i.e., instead of giving way to adverse circumstances."[2] Those that successfully weathered the test of persecution and the peril of apostasy would be guaranteed deliverance. Though some would inevitably suffer betrayal, persecution, and martyrdom, their spiritual welfare was sealed. Jesus was assuring them that regardless of whatever the world could hurl against them, even death, all that the forces of evil could ultimately accomplish was to "kill the body but not the soul." In the final analysis, no lasting harm could befall them, or as Luke figuratively puts it, "There shall not an hair of your head perish" (Luke 21:18). In reference to these two consoling assurances, Alfred Edersheim noted:

> As regards the persecutions in prospect, full Divine aid is promised to Christians—alike to individuals and to the church. Thus all care and fear may be dismissed: their testimony shall neither be silenced, nor shall the church be suppressed or extinguished; but inward joyousness, outward perseverence, and final triumph. . . . And, as for the other and equally consoling fact: despite the persecution of Jews and Gentiles, before the End cometh, this Gospel of the Kingdom shall be preached in all the inhabited earth for a testimony to all nations.[3]

"The End"

The "end" of which Christ speaks (Matthew 24:6, 13, 14) has an ultimate application to the end of this age, and the call for endurance is a challenge which falls upon Christians of every period throughout the church's history. However,

---

2. W. E. Vine, *Vine's Expository Dictionary of New Testament Words*, p. 194.
3. Alfred Edersheim, The Life and Times of Jesus the Messiah, p. 448.

though these assurances are a constant source of comfort to every believer, they had a particular bearing upon the disciples of *that* generation facing the devastating upheavals which would accompany the end of Israel's national polity. Unquestionably, His promise is to the faithful and persevering throughout the church age. But in view of the rapidly approaching destruction of Jerusalem, it had a special application to those who would weather the peculiar trials associated with that awesome event. Those trials, He intimated, would be very severe, but the Lord had provided *that* generation of believers with the consolation that "he that shall endure unto the end, the same shall be saved." In a practical sense, these comforting guarantees of deliverance were literally fulfilled as we shall see.

It should be added that some scholars have viewed these passages as strictly applying to the time period prior to 70 A.D. They see the Lord's statement that "this gospel of the kingdom shall be preached in all the world for a witness unto all nations; then the *end* shall come" (Matthew 24:14), as primarily referring to that period. They interpret the *end* as the end of the Jewish national existence in 70 A.D., rather than the end of the age. To support their position, they emphasize that the gospel had indeed gone into all the world by the time Jerusalem fell (see Romans 1:8; 16:26; Colossians 1:6; 1:23). We would agree that the gospel did in fact have a tremendous impact upon the known world in the time frame prior to Jerusalem's ruin, but in a much broader context, Jesus was revealing that the gospel would spread its triumphant influence even unto the uttermost parts of the earth before that day which marked the termination of this age.

Questions for Discussion

1. What is the greater threat to the church—the external threat of persecution, or the internal threat of false prophets? Why?

2. Do you feel that persecution is a detrimental factor in the church's experience? Why? What has history taught us concerning this?

3. List some key New Testament passages which prove that Christ did not guarantee the church immunity from persecution or tribulation.

4. Why hasn't Christ sheltered His church from the external pressures of persecution?

5. Do you feel that some end-time perspectives tend to produce a subtle form of "persecution complex" in the way Christians relate to the future? If so, discuss some of the side effects which are manifested.

6. List some so-called Christian cults which owe their formation to the effects of false prophets.

7. Do you feel that Christ's statement that the end would not come until the gospel of the kingdom is first preached *in all the world* for a witness unto every nation acts as a catalyst for evangelistic endeavors?

8. Do you agree with those scholars who maintain that Christ's assurance that "the gospel must first be preached in all the world for a witness unto all nations" was fulfilled prior to the *end* of Jerusalem in 70 A.D.? If so, what is the church's present responsibility to fulfill the Great Commission?

9. Jesus strongly cautioned His followers not to view wars, the rise of false Messiahs, famines, pestilences, or earthquakes as positive indications of the end of the world.

49

However, Christians have repeatedly pointed to these signs as proofs of the end in an attempt to forcefully challenge the lost. Should Christians capitalize upon the fear of wars and earthquakes in an attempt to win the lost, in spite of Christ's caution that these signs were not omens of the end? Can our awareness that these disturbances are not tokens of the end be used as an evangelistic tool to challenge the lost? Please explain.

"WHEN YE THEREFORE SHALL SEE"

Chapter Six

"WHEN YE THEREFORE SHALL SEE"

MATT. 24	MARK 13	LUKE 21
15 When ye therefore shall see the abomination of desolation, spoken of by Daniel the prophet, stand in the holy place, (whoso readeth, let him understand:) 16 Then let them which be in Judaea flee into the mountains:	14 But when ye shall see the abomination of desolation, spoken of by Daniel the prophet, standing where it ought not, (let him that readeth understand,) then let them that be in Judea flee to the mountains:	20 And when ye shall see Jerusalem compassed with armies, then know that the desolation thereof is nigh. 21 Then let them which are in Judea flee to the mountains and let them which are in the midst of it depart out; and let not them that are in the countries enter thereinto.

Centuries had passed since the prophet Daniel had spoken of the catastrophic events destined to befall Israel. In responding to the disciples' inquiries concerning the specific timing of Jerusalem's destruction, the Lord reached back through time to extract key prophetic statements which had a direct bearing upon the tragic events slated to transpire.

The Specific Sign

These passages mark a crucial juncture in the Lord's prophetic discourse. Thus far, the Lord has limited His comments to outlining the general signs which would typify the period preceding Israel's collapse. However, at this point, He abruptly changes the thrust of His response, as indicated by the word BUT in Mark's account. His response now focuses upon specifics, rather than generalities. He now shifts His attention to addressing the distinct sign which would precede it. The sign would be so obvious that it would be impossible for the disciples to misinterpret. It would serve to alert the Judean believers, of *that* generation, to the nearness of Jerusalem's ruin.

His information was very practical and provided His people with precise instructions on how to secure their safe deliverance before the city's destruction. This portion of the prophecy was the most important of the entire discourse, as far as the Lord's disciples in Jerusalem and Judea were concerned. It disclosed to them the distinct sign which they had requested whereby they would be alerted to the impending desolation and thereby be aided in the timing of their escape.

Prophecies in Parallel

These parallel passages constitute the pivotal point of the prophecy. An accurate interpretation at this stage of the discourse is absolutely imperative. A failure to do so will invariably result in an improper explanation of significant portions of the remainder of this prophecy.

A comparison of the three accounts at this point is extremely helpful. It should be emphasized that in each version, Jesus opens with the words, "When ye shall see" (Matthew 24:15; Mark 13:14; Luke 21:20). He responds directly to the question of "When shall these things be?" with the corresponding answer, "When ye shall see." This important lead-reply is repeated in each of the gospel accounts.

In order to obtain a proper interpretation of these passages concerning Jerusalem's destruction, we must carefully observe that the informative wording of Luke's account,

WHEN YE SHALL SEE JERUSALEM COMPASSED WITH ARMIES, then know that the desolation thereof is nigh.

specifically refers to the destruction of Jeursalem by the armies of Imperial Rome in 70 A.D. It is essential that we recognize that the distinctive wording of Luke's text corresponds to and harmonizes with Matthew and Mark's versions which also begin with the statement "WHEN YE therefore SHALL SEE" (Matthew 24:15-23; Mark 13:14-20).

53

Expositors overwhelmingly concede that Luke's account directly applies to Jerusalem's destruction in 70 A.D. This is an indisputable fact supported by the scriptural details of this text, as well as by historic reality. However, a careful correlation of Luke's version with that of Matthew and Mark's accounts clearly reveals that each is referring to this same historic event. I will show that each of the parallel accounts contains explicit details which prove that when Jesus said "When ye therefore shall see," He was directly referring to the catastrophic events which shipwrecked *that* generation of Palestinian Jews in 70 A.D., and not to a future end-time tribulation as many contend.

A parallel comparison proves Luke's version to be the master key which unlocks the exact meaning and application of Christ's response concerning the timing of Jerusalem's destruction. The distinctive details provided by Luke serves as an indispensable aid in unraveling the obscurities locked within the companion wording of Matthew and Mark's accounts. Luke's statements act as a contextual balance for Matthew's and Mark's Olivet accounts and places this division of the prophecy in its proper historical setting.

A Conflict in Wording?

Unique wording is found in each account. Though the phraseology differs slightly, a careful examination of the three versions demonstrates that the wording agrees in meaning and application. For example, Matthew's account closely parallels Mark's except that the phrase "stand in the holy place" is altered slightly to "standing where it ought not," but the essential meaning remains the same. Luke omits the mention of "Daniel the prophet" and the "holy place," but adds the necessary detail which explains and harmonizes the meaning of the other two versions.

Though the meaning of Matthew's and Mark's wording is somewhat obscure, the language of Luke's text provides sufficient explanation of the perplexing phrases employed in the other two accounts. A careful comparison of these parallel passages leaves little room for confusion or uncertainty concerning the intended meaning and application of these companion texts. Matthew's and Mark's accounts are brought into clear focus through the plain language and descriptive information employed by Luke:

> And when ye shall see JERUSALEM COMPASSED WITH ARMIES, then know that THE DESOLATION thereof is nigh. Then let them which are in Judea flee to the mountains (Luke 21:20, 21).

Furthermore, though there are distinct differences in wording, the contextual similarities connected with these parallel passages work to compatibly link them together. For example, each of the parallel accounts include the caution, "Then let them that be in Judea flee to the mountains," and each include the same identical instructions for escape. These corresponding similarities cannot be easily ignored.

The enigmatic wording of Matthew can be attributed to the apostle's desire to employ terms which individuals other than the Lord's disciples would be at a loss to decipher. Since Matthew's gospel was written mainly for circulation among the Palestinian, Jewish believers, we can understand why the Holy Spirit directed him to use veiled words which would hinder the unregenerate Jews from comprehending the specific instructions of the Lord. This would not apply to Luke's version because his gospel was primarily penned for distribution among the Gentile converts living outside the borders of Judea. There was no practical need for obscurity or concealment in the wording of Luke's version, because the specific warning "When ye therefore shall see" had little bearing upon the Gentile Christians living beyond the boundaries of Palestine. The distinctive Jewish phraseology of "the abomination of desolation" would be confusing and incomprehensible to the Gentile mind. Throughout Luke's gospel, he translates, paraphrases, or altogether omits typical Jewish names and expressions for the benefit of his Gentile readers; he purposefully avoids any hint of confusing Jewish terminology. Luke studiously strives to provide his Gentile readers with a clear, paraphrased description of the sign.

Matthew and Mark's accounts include the advice "Whoso readeth let him understand," but Luke's version omits this because the necessary explanation was clearly provided in the wording of his text. This parenthetical statement was not originally spoken by Jesus, but was inserted by Mark and Matthew in order to emphasize the urgent need for their readers to carefully consider the specific meaning of the Lord's cryptic wording, "When ye therefore shall see the abomination of desolation spoken of by Daniel the prophet, standing in the holy place . . ." (Matthew 24:15). On the other hand, Luke had no need to veil the statements of Jesus, but plainly said:

> When ye shall see Jerusalem compassed (surrounded) with armies, then know that the desolation is nigh (Luke 21:20).

The encircling of Jerusalem by the Roman legions would be the unmistakable sign which would alert the disciples to the impending desolation. Luke clearly reveals what this sign of the "abomination of desolation" was. The abomination that would make Jerusalem desolate would be the invading Gentile armies:

And when ye shall see Jerusalem compassed with ARMIES, then know that the desolation is nigh. . . . And they shall fall by the edge of the sword, and shall be led away captive into all nations: and Jerusalem shall be trodden down of the Gentiles (Luke 21:20, 24).

Daniel and 70 A.D.

Matthew and Mark point out that this "abomination of desolation" had been prophetically referred to by Daniel. Jesus had informed His followers that when they should observe the abomination of desolation positioned in the holy place, they were to recognize it to be the direct fulfillment of Daniel's prophecies (see Daniel 9:26, 27). Daniel's statements harmonize with the details provided by Luke when he stated:

. . . and the people [Romans] of the prince [Titus] that shall come shall DESTROY THE CITY [Jerusalem] and the sanctuary [temple]; and the end thereof shall be with a flood, and unto the end of the war desolations are determined (Daniel 9:26), and

. . . for the overspreading of abominations he shall make it desolate . . . [literally: with the abominable armies, He shall make it desolate] (Daniel 9:27).

A comparison of these verses with the Lord's reference to Daniel's prophecy shows that what was destined to become desolate was Jerusalem. The desolating instrument would be a hostile, heathen force. This is in keeping with the initial statements of the Lord concerning the predicted destruction of Jerusalem (Matthew 23:38; 24:2), as well as the obvious context of the Lord's response in direct reply to His disciples' question of when this would be. This was the obvious sign which would provide advance warning to God's people to facilitate their safe flight from the city.

As I've stressed, the partial wording variations in the corresponding accounts do not significantly hinder or confuse the obvious interpretation of these statements in the light of comparing these parallel passages. These accounts are proven to be complementary, and not contradictory, through a careful comparison of scripture. What Matthew's and Mark's versions lack in clarity, Luke's sufficiently makes up for in detail. Matthew's and Mark's versions speak of the *abomination of desolation,* while Luke's simply refers to the *desolation* of Jerusalem by invading armies. But a simple comparison of texts reveals that it was precisely the destruction of Jerusalem by foreign intervention which was to be the abomination. This is in harmony with the statements of the prophet Daniel concerning that which was to befall the Jewish nation ("upon thy people [Jews] and upon thy holy city [Jerusalem]," Daniel 9:24). Daniel 9:27 speaks of the overspreading of abominations which shall make it (Jerusalem) desolate. This fitly describes the spreading abroad of the Roman legions and the gradual advance of their forces. The abomination which would stand in the holy place and wreak destruction upon Jerusalem was the Roman legions and their auxiliary forces. This was the abomination that would make desolate.

"The Abomination of Desolation"

The word *abomination* is derived from the Greek *bdelugma,* and means "nausea because of stench, an object of disgust, hatred, and revulsion." The word fitly describes the feelings the Jews harbored toward the pagan Roman armies and

58

their mission of destruction. Nothing could be more detestable to the Jews than the realization that an idolatrous Gentile army was advancing to destroy their beloved city and holy sanctuary. The ensigns and images which the Roman legions carried into battle, along with their heathen sacrifices and customs were a loathsome abomination to the Jews. The Roman eagles, which served as standards for the legions, were considered to be idolatrous images specifically forbidden in the Ten Commandments. Their presence was considered to be a vile pollution of the holy city. The profaning of the temple by foreigners was viewed as the ultimate possible desecration. Their national indignation was aptly characterized by the words of Jesus when He said:

When ye shall see the abomination of desolation . . . STANDING WHERE IT OUGHT NOT . . . (Mark 13:14).

It was this encroachment of heathen armies upon the sacred soil of Israel (*where it ought not*) which was an abomination to the Jewish people.

It is interesting to note that the phrase "abomination of desolation" is better translated "the abomination that makes desolate." Some expositors have defined it as "the detestable thing causing the desolation of the holy place." Concerning the application of the expression "the abomination of desolation," Alfred Plummer added that it meant: "That which causes desolation by bringing disaster and ruin," and further adds that "heathen Rome is here indicated."[1]

The thought of idolaters desecrating the holy city was exceptionally revolting to the devout Jew in view of the past astrocities endured under the infamous hands of Antiochus

---

1. Alfred Plummer, *The Gospel According to St. Mark*, p. 298.

Epiphanes who violated the city of Jerusalem and the sanctuary in 168 B.C. He treacherously slew 40,000 Jews, plundered the temple of its sacred vessels, sacrificed a great sow upon the altar of burnt offering, and sprinkled broth from the unclean flesh all over the holy grounds for the sole purpose of defiling them. This event was a direct fulfillment of Daniel 11:31 when he referred to the "abomination that maketh desolate." Though this verse was not a direct reference to the desecration of Jerusalem by the Roman armies in 70 A.D., it was a foreshadowing of that abominable event. This event perpetrated by Antiochus Epiphanes is also mentioned in I Maccabees 1:54-57 in reference to the erection of the image of Jupiter Olympus upon the altar of burnt offering in the temple compound. This sacrilegious act left an indelible imprint upon the religious sensitivities of the Jewish nation. This historic precedent had sufficiently instilled a deep-seated sense of disgust within the Jews towards anything or anyone who would dare repeat such a spiritual atrocity. The impending reoccurrence of such an event could appropriately be called an "abomination." It is interesting to note that when the Roman legions finally subdued the city, they brought their ensigns into the temple, erected them over against the eastern gate, and sacrificed to them when they proclaimed Titus as Imperator. [2]

Standing in the Holy Place

Matthew's account states that the "abomination of desolation" would stand in the "holy place." This unique expression, found only in Matthew's version, has been the repeated grounds of controversy between expositors. Many have

2. Flavius Josephus, *Wars*, Bk. 6, Chp. 6:1.

erroneously assumed that the phrase "holy place" is a direct reference to the holy of holies in the temple. This inference has created a number of speculative theories, as we shall see. An examination of the word *place* ("holy place," Matthew 24:15) reveals that it simply means "a locality." It is the Greek word *topos* from which we extract our English words topical, topography, etc. This word is used in such biblical expressions as "a desert place" (Matthew 14:13), "dry places" (Matthew 12:43), and "stony places" (Matthew 13:20). The term *hagios topos* (*holy place*) is not applied to the holy of holies in the temple, but has a general application to the entire city of Jerusalem, as well as the holy land of Judea. Matthew Henry stated that:

> Jerusalem was the holy city, Canaan the holy land, the Mt. Moriah, which lay about Jerusalem, for its nearness to the temple was, they thought [Jews], in particular manner holy ground; on the country lying round about Jerusalem the Roman army was encamped, that was the abomination that made desolate.[3]

Adam Clarke stated that not only was the temple and the city considered to be holy, "but a considerable compass of ground about it, was deemed holy, and consequently no profane person should stand on it."[4]

In light of the interpretative perspectives I have just advocated, I maintain that the enigmatic wording of this section of the Olivet prophecy directly applies to the historic events which transpired in 70 A.D., and not to some highly speculative, futuristic setting. As I have pointed out, when the cryptic wording of Matthew's and Mark's accounts are carefully compared with the explanative wording of Luke's version, the scriptural validity of this position becomes transparent.

---

3. Matthew Henry, *Matthew Henry's Commentary*, Vol. 5, p. 352.
4. Adam Clarke, *Clarke's Commentary*, Vol. 5, p. 229.

In view of the material I have provided concerning this crucial division of the prophecy, we see that the obvious burden of proof rests upon the shoulders of futurists in attempting to place these passages in a strict, futuristic context.

Questions for Discussion

1. What are some advantages of comparing parallel material within the scriptures?
2. Explain why Luke's version is the "master key" to unlocking the interpretation of Matthew's and Mark's accounts.
3. Is there any significance in the fact that Mark's account, penned primarily for Roman readership, includes the cryptic phrase "abomination of desolation," instead of clarifying what this sign was, as Luke does?
4. Explain why Daniel 9:26, 27 tends to support the concept that the "abomination of desolation" is referring to a desolating power, rather than an idolatrous image.
5. Can you find any reasonable scriptural justification in the Olivet prophecies for applying the term "abomination of desolation" to an image of the antichrist to be erected in a rebuilt Jewish temple?
6. Some interpreters justify this belief by referring to II Thessalonians 2:4. But is this verse speaking of a rebuilt Jewish temple? Can you list any other interpretations of this verse? What does New Testament teaching say about the word "temple"? Does it refer to a literal temple, or the church?

FUTURE OR FULFILLED?

Chapter Seven

FUTURE OR FULFILLED?

Shakespeare once penned, "To be or not to be, that is the question." How fitting a question when considered in the light of the passages we've just examined. Many have already solved this problem by forcing *the abomination of desolation* into a strictly futuristic setting. However, not all agree that these excerpts from Daniel are "To be or not to be?"

Those who stress that this section of the Olivet discourse has a strictly futuristic application claim that the *abomination of desolation* will be an idolatrous image which will be erected in a rebuilt temple in Jerusalem. This belief is based upon the assumption that the phrase *holy place* is a reference to a future Jewish temple. It is a common contention that this abominable idol will be either a likeness of the antichrist, or the antichrist himself.

A Question of Weakness

In spite of the widespread popularity attending this belief, there are serious weaknesses and implausibilities which need to be considered. First of all, the setting up of a image in the holy of holies could not possibly be the sign for the disciples to flee, for this act of desecration could not happen short of armed intervention. The Jewish populace would violently resist any attempts to defile the temple at a great sacrifice of life and property. By the time the invaders seized the temple compound, Jerusalem would be surrounded and any remaining avenues of escape cut off. This would make it impossible for the disciples to flee simply because most of them would have been hopelessly trapped in the encirclement and would have been slaughtered in the ensuing conflict.

64

Even a casual examination shows that in order for something to effectively serve as an early warning for the disciples to escape, it would have to be a clear sign which would appear before a forceful penetration of the city even commenced. The sign could not possibly appear after the city had been forcefully seized, for at this point, it would be too late for the Christian community; however, the presence of heathen troops gradually approaching the city of Jerusalem would be an unmistakable sign for the disciples to flee, as was the historical case. Therefore, it is clear that the placing of an idolatrous image in the temple could not logically be the *abomination of desolation*.

Matthew's and Mark's accounts instruct the disciples to flee to the mountains at the first appearance of the *abomination of desolation* standing in the holy place. The *abomination* was to be clearly visible to the disciples both in Jerusalem and the surrounding Judean countryside. Obviously, if Jesus was referring to an image placed in the inner sanctuary, it would be hidden from the view of the entire population of Jerusalem and Judea. The only person in all Israel who had access to the holy of holies was the High Priest, and that on only one day out of the entire year. However, the plain wording of Luke's account reveals that the sign was to be clearly observed by the population of Jerusalem and Judea: "When ye shall SEE Jerusalem compassed with armies . . . then let them which are in Judea flee" (Luke 21:20, 21). What is more, Luke not only reveals the exact nature of the sign, but he includes the same, identical instructions for escape which Matthew and Mark's accounts provide.

Jesus referred to the sign as *the abomination of desolation*. Luke also mentions the appearance of the sign (Jerusalem compassed with armies) in conjunction with the city's

65

destruction. It was this abomination which was responsible for making Jerusalem a desolation. This is precisely what the Roman forces accomplished. The belief that the *abomination* is to be an idolatrous image erected in the temple is filled with contradictions, particularly in light of the fact that it was this very abomination which was to destroy the temple. Even simple logic dictates that an idol could not be set up in the temple if the temple had already been destroyed.

A Rebuilt Temple?

Many maintain that the actual temple in question is not Herod's Temple but a future temple. They insist that the temple in Jerusalem will have to be rebuilt in order for the prophecy concerning the "abomination of desolation" to be fulfilled. But forcing this assumption into the mainstream of the Olivet prophecy constitutes a violation of context. We must first ask to what temple was Jesus referring? What temple was the subject of His prophetic discourse that day? Was He speaking of the literal temple which He had specifically pointed to and declared, "Verily I say unto you, there shall not be left here one stone upon another that shall not be thrown down" (Matthew 23:2), or was He subtly referring to a rebuilt temple in Jerusalem 2,000 years later? If Jesus was referring to a future temple in which an idolatrous likeness of the antichrist will be erected, then logic requires that another Jewish sanctuary must be constructed on the site of the former structure. But this injects a totally different temple into the midst of Christ's prophetic discourse than the one concerning which the disciples inquired.

Are we to assume that when the disciples sought a clearer explanation from Jesus concerning His declaration that

Herod's Temple would be destroyed, He responded by referring to a futuristic temple? Is it reasonable to assume that Christ's temple comments actually involved a structure constructed two millenniums later—that a totally different structure was really at the heart of Christ's thoughts that day? The contextual problems with this assumption are all too apparent. This conclusion makes the discourse hopelessly confusing and totally distorts the obvious context of Christ's statements. "The prediction was perfectly clear. There was nothing veiled about it. There was no perplexing figure of speech. His language referred to the actual building and the stones. It was clear and definite."[1] The scriptures clearly specify which temple Jesus was speaking of and pointing to:

> . . . SEEST THOU *THESE* GREAT BUILDINGS? There shall not be left one stone upon another that shall not be thrown down (Mark 13:2).

Furthermore, in response to Jesus' startling declaration that *that* temple would be destroyed, the disciples pointedly asked Him when this would be. The Bible flatly states: "And Jesus ANSWERED . . ." (Matthew 24:4). However, the prophetic position of many implies that He didn't, for when the apostles raised the question concerning the destruction of the existing temple, they claim that Jesus responded by talking about a completely different structure not even in existence. If their perspective is true, then Jesus never really answered the disciples' question which the Bible says He did. Such assumptions are hopelessly misleading and confusing. Those who claim the Olivet prophecy refers to a future temple are at a complete loss to show one verse in

---

1. G. Campbell Morgan, *Studies in the Four Gospels, Luke*, p. 236.

this chapter where Jesus ever answered these questions. The only structure mentioned in Christ's prophetic reply concerned the literal temple existing in His day, and any attempts to read another building into the context of His discourse constitutes a breach of sound exegesis.

The Holy Place?

Another challenge to the rebuilt temple theory is the objection that God could conceivably refer to such a structure as *the holy place.* There was absolutely nothing holy about the temple after Christ's final impeachment of the religious authorities: "Behold your house is left unto you desolate" (Matthew 23:38). As far as Christ was concerned, it was an empty structure which He publicly disavowed any further identification with. There could be nothing holy about a rebuilt temple either. In view of God's judgment upon the temple in 70 A.D., it is highly improbable that He will ever permit the Jewish people to reconstruct another temple and reinstitute the profanity of blood sacrifices. For the Jews to mend the rent veil (Matthew 27:51) of the holy of holies, and return to their empty sacrifices and ceremonies following the crucifixion of Christ was an abominable act which held the sacrifice of God's Son in open contempt. Are we on solid scriptural ground when we teach that God will allow the Jews to reinstitute such sacrileges?

All vestiges of sacredness and holiness associated with the temple, its priesthood, sacrifices, and its ceremonies were abolished at Calvary. Though God tolerated a probationary period of 40 years for Israel, their defiant continuance in iniquity was terminated by the awesome wrath of God in 70 A.D. Since the resurrection, the only temple in which God dwells and refers to as *holy* is the church of Jesus Christ (Ephesians 2:21), a building not made with the hands but comprised of the living stones of God's people (see Acts 7:48, 49; 17:24; I Corinthians 3:9, 16; Ephesians 2:20-22; I Peter 2:5).

In closing, it is my opinion that the teaching of a rebuilt temple is founded more upon the sands of conjecture, than the reliable bedrock of scriptural reality. However, while I disagree with what I consider to be shallow assumptions on this point, I am not contending that there will not be a rebuilt Jewish sanctuary in Jerusalem—this is a moot issue. Whether or not the Jews ever manage to rebuild their temple is beside the point. The point I am making is that the temple which Jesus spoke of was directly referring to the existing one in His day, and not to some speculative temple in the future. Furthermore, His prophetic comments, at this point, were a direct response to the disciples' question regarding the precise timing of that temple's destruction which transpired in 70 A.D.

Questions for Discussion

1. Is it reasonable to assume that Christ would respond to the disciples' question about the timing of the temple's destruction by subtly referring to a futuristic temple not even in existence? Do you feel the Lord would respond in such an evasive and misleading manner?
2. In considering the principles of context, do you feel it is warranted to insert another temple into the mainstream of Christ's discourse, other than the one actually existing in His day? If so, why?
3. Why is there such an overwhelming tendency to force prophetic fulfillment into a futuristic context?
4. In light of the fact that God so decisively terminated the Levitical system of ceremonies and sacrifice, do you believe God will ever permit the Jews to rebuild their temple and resume blood sacrifices?

ARE THE THREE ACCOUNTS THE SAME DISCOURSE?

Chapter Eight

ARE THE THREE ACCOUNTS
THE SAME DISCOURSE?

In attempting to evade the problems arising from a parallel comparison of the Olivet accounts, some have devised the novel theory that Matthew's and Mark's discourses are totally different than Luke's corresponding version. They hold that there were actually two distinct Olivet discourses. While they readily accept the fact that Luke's version directly applies to the destruction of Jerusalem in 70 A.D., they maintain that Matthew's and Mark's accounts are in reference to a future tribulation which will befall Israel in the last days.

However, this argument subtly works to support the position I have taken, for if Luke's version can be proven to be the same as Matthew's and Mark's, then the *great tribulation* mentioned in these accounts is actually in reference to the fall of Jerusalem, and the *abomination of desolation* spoken of by Daniel the prophet is none other than the Roman armies under Titus. Those who take the position that Luke's version is an entirely different discourse recognize that if the three accounts can be proven to be the same, then much of their futuristic system of interpretation collapses.

Each of the Olivet prophecies was delivered shortly after Christ's triumphant entry into Jerusalem (Matthew 21:1-11; Mark 11:1-11; Luke 19:29-44). In each account, He had recently purged the temple of the moneychangers (Matthew 21:12, 13; Mark 11:15-17; Luke 19:45, 46). According to each of the gospel accounts, the Olivet discourse occurred just after Christ had exited the temple for the last time. In each case, He had just delivered a scathing rebuke against the religious authorities. In Mark's and Luke's accounts, He had just concluded commenting on the poor widow and her

71

two mites as He was leaving the temple compound (see Mark 12:41-44 and Luke 21:1-4). In each account, as the disciples admired the grandeur of the temple, the Lord revealed that "there shall not be left one stone upon another, that shall not be thrown down" (Matthew 24:2; Mark 13:2; Luke 21:6). In each account, the Olivet prophecy was given in direct response to the disciples' inquiries concerning "When shall these things be?" What is more, Luke's account follows the same order as the others, and records many of the same passages and exact wording.

In light of these glaring facts, we must conclude that it would be highly improbable for the Lord to have given two distinct Olivet discourses on the same day, following the same events, and in direct reply to the same questions, from the same disciples. Furthermore, why would Luke speak so explicitly of the impending destruction of Jerusalem in 70 A.D. and the ensuing worldwide dispersion of the Jews, and totally omit any reference to a far worse tribulation reserved for the last days, which is the primary interpretative thrust of Matthew's and Mark's discourse as futuristic expositors contend? Moreover, in view of the prominence given by Luke to the approaching destruction of Jerusalem, why would Matthew and Mark ignore such a catastrophic event and describe in identically the same context another tribulation in the distant future?

A careful contextual comparison of these Olivet accounts overwhelmingly proves that they are all speaking of the same historical event which Luke so aptly described. The proofs are absolutely conclusive that each of the three versions refer to one and the selfsame discourse uttered by the Lord. They amply support the contention that there was only one Olivet prophecy delivered by Christ.

Questions for Discussion

1. What significance is there in the fact that the Mount Olivet discourse was recorded in three separate versions?

2. Could you find any other scriptural supports which prove that the three accounts are the same discourse?

3. Using scripture, could you offer a valid defense supporting the position that Luke's account is not the same as Matthew's and Mark's?

4. Does the fact that some dispensationalists go to great lengths to deny that Luke's account is the same as Matthew's and Mark's indicate some inherent weakness in their method of interpreting the Olivet prophecy, or indicate a prophetic bias which has a negative impact upon their sound interpretation of this discourse? Please explain.

5. In light of the fact that Matthew's account was written primarily for the Jewish reader, why would Matthew, according to futurists, totally ignore such an important issue as Jerusalem's destruction, and describe in identically the same context another tribulation at the end of this age?

6. Is it conceivable that God would refer to such a rebuilt temple as the "holy place"? According to New Testament teaching, which temple does God now dwell in and call holy?

7. What would be the impact upon the gospel if the Jews were permitted to reinstate the old covenant of sacrifices?

8. Do you see a fulfillment of Daniel's statement that the sacrifices and oblations would cease (Dan. 9:27) with the end of the Levitical system in 70 A.D.? If not, how

do you reconcile his statement with the fact that the entire sacrificial system was obliterated with the destruction of Jerusalem in 70 A.D.?

9. Dispensationalists claim that the abomination of desolation will be an image of the antichrist set up in a rebuilt, Jewish temple. Is it reasonable to assume that the Jews would permit such a sacrilege without intense resistance and bloodshed?

10. Why did God allow a forty year probationary period for Israel before pouring out His judgment in 70 A.D.?

THE PLAN OF ESCAPE

Chapter Nine

THE PLAN OF ESCAPE

MATT. 24	MARK 13	LUKE 21
16 Then let them which be in Judaea flee into the mountains:	14 . . . then let them that be in Judaea flee to the mountains:	21 Then let them which are in Judaea flee to the mountains; and let them which are in the midst of it depart out; and let not them that are in the countries enter thereinto.
17 Let him which is on the housetop not come down to take any thing out of his house:	15 And let him that is on the housetop not go down into the house, neither enter *therein*, to take any thing out of his house:	
18 Neither let him which is in the field return back to take his clothes.	16 And let him that is in the field not turn back again for to take up his garment.	22 For these be the days of vengeance, that all things which are written may be fulfilled.
19 And woe unto them that are with child, and to them that give suck in those days!	17 But woe to them that are with child, and to them that give suck in those days!	23 But woe unto them that are with child, and to them that give suck, in those days! for there shall be great distress in the land, and wrath upon this people.
20 But pray ye that your flight be not in the winter, neither on the sabbath day:	18 And pray ye that your flight be not in the winter.	

When the Roman detachments began their advance upon Jerusalem, the Christians in the city, as well as in the surrounding countryside, were to flee in haste. The appearance of *the abomination of desolation* was the sign for precipitate flight from Judea. Luke also warned the disciples not to enter the city after the appearance of the sign lest they be trapped in the ensuing battle.

Run for Your Lives!

The urgent need for instant flight can be observed in the Lord's instructions. Those on the housetops were warned against descending into their dwellings to salvage their belongings. Such frantic actions would have immediately aroused the suspicions of the populace, and the ensuing panic would have impeded their safe exodus from the city. Instead, they were cautioned to pursue the quickest route of escape. Jewish houses within the walled cities were usually flat-roofed structures, sandwiched together, forming a continuous

76

terrace extending to the outer walls of the city. They could expedite their flight by following this elevated highway to the gates of the city.

Each of the Olivet accounts includes the comment:

Woe unto them that are with child, and to them that give suck in those days!

Luke supplies the reason for this statement:

For there shall be great distress in the land [Judea] and wrath upon this people [the Jews] (Luke 21:22).

Jesus was forewarning the disciples that those women who were with child or nursing children would be in a restrictive condition which could potentially hamper their speedy escape. These words also revealed the severity of affliction which would attend Jerusalem's desolation.

Pray!

The disciples were told to pray that their flight "be not in the winter," lest the unfavorable weather and shorter days hinder their escape. Winter rains would swell the streams and make the fields and roads impassable. The harsh weather and winter temperatures would have made their mountain hideaways unbearable.

Matthew's version, written specifically for the Jews, includes the additional instruction for the disciples to pray that their flight be not on the Sabbath day (Matthew 24:20). Jesus recognized that many of the Christians would still be "zealous of the law" (see Acts 21:20) and would have serious reservations about transgressing the Sabbath restrictions. In this case, the scruples of Jewish believers could work to hinder their safe flight and so jeopardize their very lives.

Those believers who were not conscientiously bound by these traditions also needed to pray that their flight would not fall upon the Sabbath. The observance of multitudes of people breaking the Sabbath restrictions in an attempt to flee the city would generate a great deal of suspicion among the Jewish populace. Such unlawful movements were guaranteed to arouse the indignation and resistance of the Jews.

These specific warnings were given for the sole purpose of sparing Christians from the approaching holocaust. It is important to note that these urgent instructions of Jesus were explicitly followed by the Christians of Judea and Jerusalem. Miraculously, not a single believer perished in the holocaust which engulfed Jerusalem in 70 A.D. Shortly before the city had been attacked by Titus, the Christian community, under the leadership of Symeon, a cousin of the Lord, withdrew to the village of Pella in Perea which lay in the mountainous regions east of the Sea of Galilee.

The Mysterious Retreat of Cestius Gallus

The events surrounding this safe exodus were quite extraordinary. When the Jewish uprising broke out in 66 A.D., the Roman general Cestius Gallus marched his army from Syria into Judea, laying waste to everything in his path. So rapid was his progress that he quickly invested the city and was on the verge of capturing it. The Roman assault was so swift that the Christians were prevented from escaping. They were alerted by the obvious appearance of the predicted sign of Gentile armies surrounding the city, but their exodus was prevented by the encirclement. However, a strange event occurred which contributed to the deliverance of the Christians within the city. Cestius' progress was so successful that the Jewish populace was about to capitulate and throw open the gates when suddenly, "without any reason in the world,"[1] he unexpectedly recalled his troops and withdrew from the city. This decision, totally unaccountable from any logical viewpoint, could only be attributed to the sovereign intervention of God. Had the city been captured, the city and temple would have been spared and it was neither God's intent to spare the city and sanctuary, or allow the possible annihilation of the Christians locked within it.

This mysterious retreat provided the opportunity for escape. The interval before the Roman forces returned in fury was wisely redeemed by the believers in securing their safe exodus. The Christian historian Eusebius stated that, "The whole body . . . of the church at Jerusalem, having been commanded by a divine revelation, given to men of approved piety there before the war, removed from the city and dwelt at a certain town beyond the Jordan, called Pella."[2] After Cestius Gallus had raised the siege and Vespasian was approaching with his armies, all who believed in Christ left Jerusalem and fled to Pella and other places beyond the river Jordan, marvelously escaping the general shipwreck of their country—not one of them perished!

Had the Christian community failed to respond to these clear instructions, they would likewise have perished in the siege which consumed the city in 70 A.D. Josephus states that had Cestius "continued the siege a little longer," he would certainly have taken the city, in which case the city and temple would have been spared; but he adds: "It was, I suppose, owing to the aversion God had already towards the city and the sanctuary, that he [Cestius] was hindered

---

1. Flavius Josephus, *Wars*, Bk. 2, Chp. 19:6.
2. Eusebius, Ecclesiastical History, III, 5:3.

from putting an end to the war that very day."³ The translator of Josephus added:

> There may be another very important and very providential reason assigned for this strange and foolish retreat of Cestius, (which, if Josephus had been at the time of writing his history a Christian, he might probably have taken notice of also), and that is the opportunity afforded the Jewish Christians in the city, of calling to mind the prediction and caution given them by Christ that when they should see "the abomination of desolation" (the idolatrous Roman armies, with the images of their idols in their ensigns) ready to lay Jerusalem desolate, "stand where it ought not," or "in the holy place," or when they should "see Jerusalem compassed with armies," they should then "flee to the mountains." By complying with which, those Jewish Christians fled to the mountains of Perea, and escaped this destruction. Nor was there perhaps any one instance of a more unpolitic, but more providential conduct, than this retreat of Cestius visible during this whole siege of Jerusalem, which (siege) was providentially such a "great tribulation as had not been from the beginning of the world to that time; no, nor ever shall be.⁴

Questions for Discussion

1. Does the wording of these passages lend themselves more to a first century setting, or a 20th century setting? Please explain.
2. Does the fact that Christ's warning was literally fulfilled by the church and verified by reliable witnesses offer a

---

3. Falvius Josephus, *Wars*, Bk. 2, Chp. 19:6.
4. *Ibid.*

forceful argument against a futuristic application? If not, why?

3. Does Christ's exhortation to pray say anything about the Christian's responsibility when facing approaching calamities?

4. Christ admonished the disciples against hindering their escape by returning to their homes to retrieve belongings. Does this say anything to us about our priorities? Please explain.

5. In light of the historic fulfillment of these passages, can you find any other passages which clearly teach of a coming period of great tribulation at the end of this age?

"FOR THEN SHALL BE GREAT TRIBULATION"

Chapter Ten

"FOR THEN SHALL BE GREAT TRIBULATION"

MATT. 24	MARK 13	LUKE 21
21 For then shall be great tribulation, such as was not since the beginning of the world to this time, no, nor ever shall be.	19 For in those days shall be affliction, such as was not from the beginning of the creation which God created unto this time, neither shall be.	22 For these be the days of vengeance, that all things which are written may be fulfilled. 23 But woe unto them that are with child, and to them that give suck, in those days! for there shall be great distress in the land, and wrath upon this people. 24 And they shall fall by the edge of the sword, and shall be led away captive into all nations: and Jerusalem shall be trodden down of the Gentiles, until the times of Gentiles be fulfilled.

"For then shall be great tribulation such as was not since the beginning of the world. . . ." What are we to make of this prophetic statement? Are these words a sobering glimpse of the future? When we consider the awesome calamities which have already befallen the last two millennia, we wonder what could possibly lie ahead. What could surpass the intensity of two world wars, the butchery of countless conflicts, the staggering toll of millions who have perished in famines, epidemics, and natural catastrophies? Will the world soon be plunged into a final period of unprecedented suffering which will eclipse anything in history? Are we now awaiting "The Great Tribulation," or has it already happened? These are questions we will now consider.

The Lord had previously outlined the general distresses which would emerge before Israel's destruction: wars, rumors of wars, famines, pestilences, earthquakes, and spiritual imposters. But when they saw the specific sign of "Jerusalem compassed with armies," they were warned to flee in haste.

He had given explicit instructions to spare His followers from the agonies which would engulf the nation of Israel. The ordeal would be so awesome that the disciples were warned to abandon everything and flee for their lives lest they delay or impede their escape. The Lord's instructions were delivered in the awareness that these were to be *the days of vengeance* and *wrath* which were to be executed upon that stiffnecked and rebellious generation.

God had repeatedly extended His mercy to the nation and had suffered long with their defiance, but the time was rapidly approaching when the outpouring of wrath could no longer be restrained. Christ had specified that very generation had filled the cup of God's wrath to full brim (Matthew 23:32). It was the time of divine retribution for the corporate sins of Israel (see I Thessalonians 2:14-16). It was the time for the Jewish people to "fall by the edge of the sword" and "be led away captive into all the world" (Luke 21:24). So great would be the horrors accompanying this tragic chapter in Israel's history that the Lord described it as a time of "great tribulation, such as was not since the beginning of the world to this time, no, nor ever shall be" (Matthew 24:21; see also Mark 13:19).

Unless we completely ignore the context of these statements in comparison with Luke's parallel account, the *tribulation* and *affliction* (the same Greek word, *thlipsis*) mentioned in Matthew and Mark's accounts is the same event referred to by Luke as "the days of vengeance," "great distress," and "wrath upon this people" (Luke 21:22, 23). This period of great tribulation engulfing the Jewish nation extended throughout the Jewish revolt of 66-70 A.D. and climaxed in its greatest fury with the destruction of Jerusalem and the burning of the temple by the Roman armies.

Great Tribulation!

The severity of this historic event has been attested to by the comments of numerous scholars. Shepard commented: "Greater affliction the world had never seen—would never see—than that reserved for the inhabitants of Jerusalem in that day."[1] Adam Clarke wrote:

> No history can furnish us with a parallel to the calamities and miseries of the Jews. . . . These were the days in which all the calamities predicted by Moses, Joel, Daniel, and other prophets, as well as those predicted by our Savior, met in one common center, and were fulfilled in the most terrible manner on that generation.[2]

Of this period of unparalled tribulation, the historian Josephus, who was an eyewitness, stated in his introduction to the Wars of the Jews: ". . . it appears to me that the misfortunes of all men from the beginning of the world, if they be compared to those of the Jews, are not so considerable as they were."[3]

Greater in Scope and Magnitude?

The timing of the "great tribulation, such as was not since the beginning of the world to this time, no, nor ever shall be," has been the repeated grounds of controversy between expositors. Many contend that this emphatic statement could not possibly refer to the catastrophe which befell Israel in 70 A.D. They forcefully claim that the world has since experienced periods of tribulations which have far exceeded the magnitude of the calamities that attended that period. They contend that the history of the world has

---

1. J.W. Shepard, *The Christ of the Gospels*, p. 517.
2. Adam Clarke, *Clarke's Commentary*, Vol. 5, p. 230.
3. Flavius Josephus, *Preface to Wars*, Sec. 4, p. 428.

witnessed tribulations on a much broader scale than those which afflicted Israel during the Jewish revolt of 66-70 A.D. They point to the horrors of W. W. I and W. W. II as examples of greater suffering. They frequently compare the agonies which the European Jews endured during the holocaust of Hitler's "final solution" as an obvious example of greater tribulation. However, though on the surface these arguments seem quite convincing, a closer examination of Christ's statements and historical fact reveals the error of this position.

It is a common mistake to assume that the *great tribulation* to which the Lord referred was to be a time of incomparable suffering, in regards to the numbers slain, the amount of property destroyed, the length of duration, or the extent of geographical coverage. As George Murray commented, "it was the nature, rather than the magnitude of the tribulation that our Lord had in mind and which he said was to be without equal in all of history."[4] It must be pointed out that the scriptures do not refer to this calamity as one that would exceed all others in scope or magnitude. Even at this point in history, no catastrophe could conceivably exceed, in magnitude, the flood where only eight souls survived!

"The Time of Jacob's Trouble"

The Lord's prediction of great tribulation was not in reference to a tribulation of greater scope and magnitude, but of a tribulation unique in quality. "The term, *such as . . .* does not refer to the statistical magnitude of the tribulation — it refers rather to the kind of tribulation."[5] This period of great tribulation would be a distinctive time of distress on

---

4. George Murray, *Millennial Studies*, p. 107.
5. Paul T. Butler, *The Gospel of Luke*, p. 481.

an unprecedented scale of suffering and intensity—a tribulation specifically resulting from God's wrath being unleashed upon His elect nation in particular (Luke 21:23). This point of understanding is absolutely crucial. This tribulation was a direct result of God's outpouring of judgment upon the nation of Israel and not upon the entire world! In reference to this unparalled time of tribulation, Boettner commented:

> There have been, of course, other periods of tribulation of suffering in which greater numbers of people were involved, and which continued for longer periods of time. But considering the physical, moral, and religious aspects, suffering never reached a greater degree of awfulness and intensity than in the siege of Jerusalem. Nor have so many people ever perished in the fall of any other city. We think of the atomic bomb that was dropped on Hiroshima as causing the greatest mass horror of anything in modern times. Yet only about one-tenth as many people were killed in Hiroshima as in the fall of Jerusalem. Add to the slaughter of such a great number the bestiality of Jew to Jew and of Roman to Jew and the anguish of a people who knew they were forsaken of God, and we see the justification for Christ's words, "For then shall be great tribulation, such as was not from the beginning of the world to this time, no, nor ever shall be."[6]

Never had a nation experienced such a concentrated degree of affliction at the hands of God. This was not to be world-wide tribulation, but one of unparalleled trouble for the nation of Israel alone. Ellicott stated, "other sieges may have witnessed, before and since, scenes of physical wretchedness equally appalling, but nothing that history records offers anything parallel to the alternations of frantic

---

6. Loraine Boettner, *The Millennium,* p. 202.

hope and frenzied despair that attended the breaking up of the faith and polity of Israel."[7]

Jeremiah's prophecy concerning "the time of Jacob's trouble" reveals the unique nature of this tribulation which was to afflict the nation of Israel. Jeremiah's wording parallels the wording of Jesus' Olivet discourse in describing the distinctive nature of this tribulation:

> Alas! for that day is great, so that *none is like it*: it is even the time of *Jacob's trouble* (Jeremiah 30:7).

The qualifying phrase *none like it* corresponds to the Olivet reference to the great tribulation when it says *such as was not*. The wording suggests the peculiar nature of this time of trouble. The phrase "the time of Jacob's trouble" isolates the application of this *great tribulation* to the Jewish nation in particular. Luke's text supports this: "Then shall be great distress in the land, and wrath upon *this people* (Jewish nation) (Luke 21:23).

The wording of Daniel's prophecy is equally explicit: "And there shall be a time of trouble *such as never was* since there was a *nation*" (Daniel 12:1). The words *such as* indicate the distinctive nature of these sufferings, and the words *since there was a nation* confine the specific application to the Jewish nation.

It should be noted that Luke flatly states that: "These be the days of vengeance THAT ALL THINGS WHICH ARE WRITTEN MAY BE FULFILLED" (Luke 21:22). Knowing that these events described by Luke apply to Jerusalem's tragic destruction in 70 A.D., we can safely conclude that it was those awesome events which marked the fulfillment of

---

7. Charles J. Ellicott, *Ellicott's Bible Commentary*, p. 739.

all the previous prophetic statements concerning the eventual judgment which was destined to befall Israel. History overwhelmingly corroborates the fulfillment of all the tragic events prophesied concerning the fall of Jerusalem and the ensuing dispersion of the surviving remnant. The numerous prophecies spoken by Moses, Daniel, Jeremiah, and even Christ found their fulfillment in 70 A.D. This period of *great tribulation* is not an event which the entire world is yet awaiting, but a past historic event of unparalled, concentrated severity specifically afflicting the Jewish nation in 70 A.D.

How Firm a Belief?

As we proceed in our examination of this crucial prophecy, I am well aware of the "entrenched" popularity attending the belief that there will be a definite period of "The Great Tribulation" preceding the visible return of Christ. The "Great Tribulation" mentioned by Christ is commonly associated with the closing years of this dispensation. This concept is so firmly established in the conviction of many that it is difficult for them to even entertain the idea that the tribulation period which the Lord referred to has long since past.

This notion is widely accepted and, for the most part, without question. Many have acquiesced to this teaching without a careful examination of the scriptures. This has often been done because of the notoriety and spiritual caliber of those who have propounded it, the belief that it was a sound tenet of eschatological teaching, or because of the erroneous assumption that it was a universally accepted position of Christian doctrine. However, in agreement with Philip Mauro, we echo his firm conviction that, "We are confident that all who are disposed to examine with open minds the testimony of the scriptures will be constrained to agree with the conclusion we have reached, which is that of practically all the great commentators of by-gone days, and of many in our own day."[8]

In conclusion, it has not been my intent to give the impression that there will be no distresses accompanying the closing days of this age. I am not questioning the fact that there will be varying degrees of tribulation during the final days of this dispensation. However, there will not be a tribulation period on the scale of magnitude and intensity as imagined by many. It is my conviction that the *great tribulation* mentioned by Christ was not in reference to a future period of end-time distress, but of a rapidly approaching event which was, as far as *that* generation of Jews was concerned, on their immediate horizon.

Furthermore, I do not believe that the Lord's response was, in any way, intended to convey a direct comparison between the severity of distresses attending the siege of Jerusalem and those which are reserved for the last days. Neither do I believe that He intended to establish any parallels whatsoever between these widely separated events. Tribulation afflicting both the world and the church has been one of the general features of this entire age. Though we have no scriptural guarantees that the last days will be any different, I do not believe that there will be the type of tribulation preceding the second coming in the unprecedented magnitude which Dispensationalists have commonly inferred from passages mentioning *great tribulation*. Concerning this wide-spread teaching of a future *great tribulation*, I agree with the pointed comments of George Murray:

---

8. Philip Mauro, *Seventy Weeks and the Great Tribulation*, p. 220.

We have read all the writing on this subject to which we had access, and have not found one absolutely convincing argument in its favor. We are therefore satisfied to believe that the tribulation here prophesied actually took place in 70 A.D. until such time as concrete and convincing scriptural evidence to the contrary is offered. We believe dipensationalism has already explored every avenue offering any possibility of this with results disappointing to itself and not convincing to others.[9]

Questions for Discussion

1. Why does it seem so logical to place a great tribulation at the close of this age?
2. In referring to timing of the great tribulation, Jesus stated that it would be "such as was not since the beginning of the world to this time, no, nor ever shall be" (Matthew 24:21). Does the qualifying phrase, "no, nor ever shall be" suggest that the great tribulation will occur at the end of this age as dispensationalists claim, or that time will continue for an indefinite period after the tribulation? Please explain what impact the latter would have on a futuristic perspective.
3. The word "great" in "great tribulation" (Matthew 24:21) can be used either intensively or extensively. How do you feel it is primarily used in the Mount Olivet discourse?
4. Dispensationalists maintain that Christ's words, "for then shall be great tribulation, such as was not since the beginning of the world to this time, no, nor ever shall be" (Matthew 24:21) prove that the great tribulation will be

---

9. George Murray, *Millennial Studies*, p. 180.

a period of unparalleled magnitude, exceeding anything in history. How do we reconcile this teaching with the magnitude and intensity of the flood?

5. Does Christ's warning for those in Jerusalem and Judea to flee indicate that the great tribulation would be a local event affecting the immediate region of Palestine, or a global event affecting the entire world?

THE TESTIMONY OF JOSEPHUS

Chapter Eleven

THE TESTIMONY OF JOSEPHUS

A Credible Witness?

Flavius Josephus (37-100 A.D.) was a Jewish author and historian who wrote a comprehensive history of the Jewish revolt (66-70 A.D.) in a book entitled "The Wars of the Jews." He was a remarkable individual who was a Jewish priest, general, author, and Roman citizen. He was actually involved in the early stages of the Jewish uprising as general of the Jewish forces opposing the Roman armies. His forces were eventually subdued by Vespasian's legions during the siege of the fortress at Jotapata in July of A.D. 67. When he was brought as a prisoner before Vespasian, he delivered an amazingly accurate prophecy predicting that Vespasian would be the next emperor. His prophecy was fulfilled two years later when Vespasian's legions proclaimed him Emperor of Rome. This prophecy helped place Josephus in a unique position of favor with Vespasian. He was subsequently freed and became a reporter, interpreter, and go-between during the final conflict at Jerusalem.

Josephus devoted nearly 200 pages of eyewitness accounts to the events surrounding the destruction of Jerusalem. His writings constitute the only detailed account that we possess of the devastating holocaust which engulfed the Jewish nation. His journal of the Jerusalem destruction attests to the incomparable suffering which the Jewish nation endured during that period of great tribulation.

It is the learned opinion of many scholars that his account of these great events has been providentially preserved for our instruction. When his book was first published in 75 A.D., the facts concerning the holocaust of 70 A.D. were

94

still vividly impressed upon the memories of many. The publication of the details of this historic event, at a time when the facts related by him were still freshly known to thousands, is strong proof of the accuracy of his information. Since Josephus was not a Christian, he cannot be accused of intentionally slanting his material to conform to the predictions of the Olivet prophecy. Yet the information of his historic chronicle works to confirm the fulfillment of Christ's prophecies concerning the *great tribulation* and *days of vengeance* which were to come upon the Jewish people and their homeland (Luke 21:23). Not only does the information which Josephus provides substantiate the reality that this was indeed a period of unique affliction unlike any that the world had ever experienced or ever would witness in the future, it also substantiates the literal accuracy of the Lord's statements concerning the impending destruction of the temple and the judgments which would befall the nation (Matthew 23:38; 24:2).

I should note that in referring to Josephus' historical sketch of the events surrounding the last days of Jerusalem and the Jewish nation, I am not attempting to interpret scripture solely through the eyes of secular history. I firmly believe that scripture is able to interpret scripture. However, as a secular document, his account is recognized to be an accurate recital of the events which he had personal acquaintance with, which he, himself, viewed as a divine fulfillment of Daniel's prophecy,[1] and which strongly corroborate the literal fulfillment of Christ's Olivet prophecy.

A Prelude to War

Israel had teetered for years on the brink of open hostilities with Rome. Roman insensitivity and tyranny had increasingly

---

1. Flavius Josephus, *Antiquities*, Bk. 10, Chp. 11:7.

contributed to the acute state of discontent festering within the Jewish nation. Clashes with the Roman authorities repeatedly drove the nation to the edge of open revolt.

The turbulent state of the Judean province was intensified by the disruptive influence of political factions within the nation. Civil disorders and chaos were constantly being fomented by seditious elements, thus escalating the instability of the times.

Roving bands of robbers and cutthroats infested the countryside, and an organized group of assassins brutalized the populace. Added to this criminal element, an increasing number of religious charlatans, fanatic zealots, and political troublemakers arose and plagued the inhabitants of Judea and Jerusalem.

In the face of such civil turbulence it is little wonder that Rome's ability to maintain any semblance of law and order steadily deteriorated. Josephus likened the social conditions to a "diseased body,"[2] for as soon as one disturbance was quelled, another immediately erupted.

The turbulence which had been brewing for years finally erupted into full scale war with Imperial Rome in 66 A.D. In the ensuing conflict, thousands of Jews were butchered throughout Palestine, Syria, and Alexandria. City after city was pillaged and the Jewish populations exterminated. The civil war raged for over three years before the Roman forces finally concentrated their fury against the last Jewish stronghold at Jerusalem.

It should be noted that in the interval after Cestius Gallus' mysterious retreat (Chapter 9), the Roman forces were engaged in subduing the provinces of Galilee and Judea for

---

2. Flavius Josephus, *Wars*, Bk. 2, Chp. 13:6.

a period of time before attacking Jerusalem. This fact aids us in understanding Matthew 24:15-21. Christ's initial warnings to flee were directed to "them which be in Judea" (Matthew 24:16; Mark 13:14; Luke 21:21). His words clearly show that the anticipated sign of *the abomination of desolation* which was predicted to stand *in the holy place* and which was to serve as a signal for *them which be in Judea to flee into the mountains* could not possibly be an idol erected in the inner sanctuary of the temple, for by this time the desolation of Judea would have already been accomplished and its inhabitants butchered.

Slaughter Within the Walls

When Vespasian turned his armies towards Jerusalem, the city was teeming with refugees who had flooded in from the ravaged countryside. They were doomed to become the hundreds of thousands of statistics in the coming siege.

Throughout the remaining struggle, the Jews suffered more from the self-inflicted atrocities imposed upon one another inside the walls than from the Romans without. Josephus added, ". . . that for barbarity and iniquity those of the same nation did in no way differ from the Romans; nay, it seemed to be a much lighter thing to be ruined by the Romans than by themselves."[3]

Multitudes of thieves, zealots, and murderers had flocked into the city, only compounding the confusion within the walls. Jerusalem was without law and order. It was a city filled with anarchy. The city was divided into warring factions who took turns in decimating one another. The fanatic zealots and the criminal elements wreaked havoc upon their

---

3. *Ibid.*, Bk. 4, Chp. 3:2.

own people. They fought one another with such malice and abandon that thousands of innocent Jews were cut down in their "cross-fire." Though they were a small minority in comparison to the hundreds of thousands hemmed within the city, they terrorized the people and ruthlessly murdered any who stood in their way. They treacherously attacked the peaceful elements and indiscriminately slaughtered both young and old. Even the priesthood was not exempt from their barbarity. The nobles and peaceful citizenry who refused to cooperate with the zealots' demands were also brutally tortured and slain. Over 12,000 of the more eminent inhabitants perished in this manner.

All who sought to escape the city had their throats slit, if caught by the zealots, and their bodies left to rot. Because of the numbers slain, burial became an impossibility. Great heaps of cadavers were piled in the city, trampled over, or thrown from the city's walls.

Josephus noted that the warring factions were "agreed in nothing but to kill those that were innocent," and added,

> the noise of those that were fighting was incessant, both by day and by night; but the lamentations of those that mourned exceeded the noise of the fighting. . . . They, moreover, were continually inventing pernicious things against each other; and when they had resolved upon anything, they executed it without mercy, and omitted no method of torment or of barbarity. [4]

In view of these distresses, we can understand the appropriateness of Jesus' words when he said,

> Daughters of Jerusalem, weep not for me, but for yourselves, and for your children (Luke 23:28).

---

4. *Ibid.*, Bk. 5, Chp. 1:5.

At this point in the Jewish revolt, the Romans had not yet reached the city in force, and because the Passover season had arrived and there seemed to be a momentary lull in the hostilities, the gates of the city were thrown open for all those who desired to observe the feast. It was this act which helped to swell the number of people within the city and which contributed to the tremendous slaughter which was to take place. William Whiston, the translator of Josephus, adds in a footnote:

> Here we see the true occasion of those vast numbers of Jews that were in Jerusalem during the siege by Titus, and perished therein; that the siege began at the Feast of Passover, when such prodigious multitudes of Jews and proselytes were come from all parts of Judea, and from other countries.[5]

It is interesting to note that the Christians of Judea did not avail themselves of this false opportunity for security. This was in direct response to the Lord's caution not to enter the city at the appearance of the sign (Luke 21:21), lest they be trapped in the ensuing holocaust.

The Jews were so persistent in their fanatical acts of fratricide that even when the Roman legions finally ringed the city and fully engaged the Jewish defenders, the internal dissension between the seditious factions did not cease:

> They returned to their former madness, and separated one from another, and fought it out; and they did everything that the besiegers (Romans) could desire them to do. For they never suffered anything that was worse from the Romans than they made each other suffer; nor was there any misery endured by the city after these men's actions that could be esteemed new. . . . For I venture to say that the sedition

---

5. Flavius Josephus, *Wars*, Bk. 5, Chp. 3:1.

destroyed the city, and the Romans destroyed the sedition. This was a much harder thing to do than to destroy the walls. So that we may justly ascribe our misfortunes to our own people.[6]

He further stated,

I cannot but speak my mind . . . and it is this: I suppose that had the Romans delayed their coming against these villains, the city would either have been swallowed up by the ground opening upon them, or been overflowed by water, or else been destroyed by such thunder as the country of Sodom perished by, for it had brought forth a generation of men much more atheistical than those that suffered such punishments; for by their madness it was that all the people came to be destroyed.[7]

This internal discord contributed more to the final destruction of Jerusalem than the Roman armies besieging it.

At this stage in the conflict, Vespasian was recalled to Rome because of Nero's death, and was soon proclaimed Emperor himself. The responsibility of quenching the Jewish revolt now fell upon the shoulders of his son, Titus.

Though the Jews continued murdering one another, they also offered stiff resistance to the Roman forces. However, in spite of their stubborn resistance, Titus repeatedly offered clemency to the inhabitants within the city if they would but lay down their arms. He dispatched Josephus before the walls of the city to appeal to the Jewish defenders and exhort them to yield before it was too late. In an impassioned plea, Josephus reasoned with them of the futility of resisting the power of Rome, and stated that "God was no longer with them." But the appeals of mercy fell on deaf ears and

---

6. Flavius Josephus, *Wars*, Bk. 5, Chp. 6:2.
7. *Ibid.*, Chp. 13:6.

only incensed the obstinate Jews and stiffened their resolve to resist the Romans. His repeated attempts to stop the needless slaughter and spare the city were futile. Josephus offered a sobering comment on this point: "In reality, it was God who condemned the whole nation, and turned every course that was taken for their preservation, to their destruction."[8] They had sealed their fate.

The Famine

In the course of these constant battles between the divisive factions, the city's granaries and storehouses, which contained enough provisions to sustain the population for several years, were deliberately torched. The water reservoirs were also polluted to keep others from having them. The destruction of such a vast quantity of food reserves was the direct occasion of a terrible famine which consumed the city. The ensuing famine claimed immense numbers of Jews during Jerusalem's siege.

As the battle raged without the walls, the sedition and famine spread within the city.

> The madness of the seditions did also increase together with their famine, and both those miseries were everyday inflamed more and more; for there was no corn that appeared anywhere publicly . . . it was now a miserable case, and a sight that would justly bring tears into our eyes . . . insomuch that children would pull the very morsels that their fathers were eating out of their mouths . . . so did mothers do to their infants.[9]

Many sold their homes, their children, and anything they possessed for one measure of wheat or barley. Some were

---

8. *Ibid.*, Chp. 13:5.
9. *Ibid.*, Chp. 10:2, 3.

so desperate that they ate from public sewers, cattle and pigeon dung, wood, leather shields, hay, clothing, and things that scavenger animals would not eat!

The seditious factions ravaged the city in their constant search for provisions to sustain themselves in the siege, and "they invented terrible methods of torment to discover where any food was."[10] Unbelievable forms of torture were inflicted upon those suspected of concealing food. Josephus commented on their cruelty:

> It is impossible to give every instance of the iniquity of these men. I shall therefore speak my mind here at once briefly: that neither did any other city suffer such miseries, nor did any age ever breed a generation more fruitful in wickedness than this was, from the beginning of the world.[11]

As the effects of the famine intensified, multitudes of Jews left the city at night to forage the valleys surrounding the walls for food. The Romans captured thousands and crucified them on stakes in plain sight of the defenders upon the walls at a rate of over 500 a day. So many were killed in this manner that "room was wanting for crosses, and crosses wanting for bodies."[12]

Josephus' observation amazingly parallels the prophecy of Jesus that these *days of affliction* were to surpass anything the world had ever witnessed previously (Mark 13:19). His testimony attests to the unique nature of this great tribulation. No nation has ever suffered such a degree of "self-inflicted" torments than that nation experienced.

---

10. *Ibid.*, Chp. 10:3.
11. *Ibid.*, Chp. 10:5.
12. *Ibid.*, Chp. 11:1.

The Noose Is Tightened

After having attempted several unsuccessful assaults upon
the city, Titus ordered his troops to surround the city with
a wall in order to cut off any remaining avenues of escape.
This feat was accomplished in only three days, and was an
accurate fulfillment of Christ's prediction when He said:

> Thine enemies shall cast a trench about thee, and compass
> thee round, and keep thee on every side (Luke 19:43).

It is interesting to note that of the twenty-seven sieges against
Jerusalem, this was the only one in which the city was surrounded by a wall.

The total encirclement of the city greatly intensified the
famine's progress:

> Then did the famine widen its progress, and devoured the
> people by whole houses and families; the upper rooms were
> filled with women and children dying of the famine; and the
> lanes of the city were full of the dead bodies of the aged;
> the children also and the young men wandered about the
> market places like shadows, all swelled with famine, and
> fell down dead wherever their misery seized them.[13]

> Thus did the miseries of Jerusalem grow worse and worse
> every day . . . and indeed the multitude of carcases that
> lay in heaps one upon another was a horrible sight, and
> produced a pestilential stench, which was a hindrance to
> those that would make sallies out of the city and fight the
> enemy.[14]

> Now of those that perished by famine in the city, the number
> was prodigious, and the miseries they underwent were un-
> speakable; for if so much of any kind of food did anywhere
> appear, a war was commenced presently; and the dearest

13. *Ibid.*, Chp. 12:3.
14. *Ibid.*, Bk. 6, Chp. 1:1.

friends fell fighting one with another over it, snatching from each other the most miserable supports of life.[15]

So bitter were the distresses caused by the famine that Josephus relates the story of one eminent woman who

slew her son: and then roasted him, and ate half of him, and kept the other half by her concealed. When the seditious Jews came in search for food, having smelled the "horrid scent," they threatened her that they would cut her throat if she did not shew them what food she had. . . . She replied that she had saved a very fine portion for them. When she uncovered the remains of her son, they were seized with horror and amazement of mind, and stood astonished at the sight; when she said to them, "Come, eat of this food; for I have eaten of it myself. Do not you pretend to be more tender than a woman, or more compassionate than a mother. With these words, they fled in utter terror and upon which the whole city was full of the horrors which the woman had done."[16]

TITUS

In a final, desperate attempt to elicit the Jews' surrender before the city and temple were destroyed, Titus dispatched Josephus to urge the defenders to cease their senseless resistance. But his words were again rejected. Josephus concluded his appeal with his sobering epitaph upon the nation: "It is God therefore, it is God himself who is bringing this fire, to purge this city, which

---

15. *Ibid.*, Bk. 6, Chp. 3:3.
16. *Ibid.*, Chp. 3:4.

is full of your pollutions."[17] The translator of Josephus added his observation concerning this statement of Josephus:

> Josephus speaks so, that it is most evident he was fully satisfied that God was on the Roman's side, and made use of them for the destruction of the Jews, which was for certain the true state of this matter, as the prophet Daniel first, and our Savior himself afterwards had clearly foretold.[18]

The Wall Is Breached

Finally the wall was breached, and in spite of Titus' strict orders, the temple was torched by his enraged soldiers. Josephus relates:

> But as for that house [temple], God had for certain long ago doomed it to the fire; and now that fatal day was come, according to the revolution of ages. It was the tenth day of the month Ab, the day upon which it was formerly burnt by the King of Babylon.[19]

He further says:

> While the holy house was on fire, everything was plundered that came to hand, and ten thousand of those that were caught were slain. Nor was there commiseration of any age, or any reverence of gravity; but children, old men, profane persons, and priests were all slain in the same manner. . . . Moreover, many, when they saw the fire, exerted their utmost strength, and did break out into groans and outcries. Perea also did return the echo, as well as the mountains round about Jerusalem, and augmented the force of

---

17. *Ibid.*, Chp. 2:1.
18. *Ibid.*, Chp. 2:1.
19. *Ibid.*, Chp. 4:5.

the noise. Yet was the misery itself more terrible than this disorder. For one would have thought that the hill itself, on which the temple stood, was seething hot, as if full of fire on every part, that the blood was more in quantity than the fire, and that the slain were more in numbers than they who slew them. For the ground did nowhere appear visible because of the dead bodies that lay upon it.[20]

In describing the slaughter of about six thousand people who had followed the assurances of a false prophet and taken refuge in one of the cloisters near the temple, Josephus says:

A false prophet was the occasion of the destruction of those people, who had made a public proclamation in the city that very day, that God commanded them to get upon the temple, and that there they should receive miraculous signs of their deliverance. Now there was then a great number of false prophets suborned by the tyrants to impose upon the people, who denounced this to them, that they should wait for deliverance from God; and this was in order to keep them from deserting, and that they might be buoyed up above fear and care by such hopes . . . thus were the miserable people persuaded by these deceivers . . . while they did not attend, nor give credit to the signs that were so evident that did so plainly foretell their future desolation.[21]

This was an accurate fulfillment of Christ's warning concerning the appearance of false prophets in conjunction with Jerusalem's siege (see Matthew 24:23-26).

When the Romans finally penetrated the main portions of the city, the soldiers could not be restrained from ruthlessly butchering the populace. They indulged in the slaughter

---

20. *Ibid.*, Chp. 5:1.
21. *Ibid.*, Chp. 5:2, 3.

until the soldiers "grew weary of killing." Josephus stated that the soldiers,

> went into the lanes of the city with their swords drawn and slew those whom they overtook without mercy, and set fire to the houses whither the Jews had fled, and burnt every soul in them . . . they ran everyone through whom they met with, and obstructed the very lanes with their dead bodies, and made the whole city run down with blood, to such a degree indeed that the fire of many houses was quenched with these men's blood![22]

The Final Solution

When the siege was over, Titus entered Jerusalem and toured the ruins, observing the massive bulwarks of the Jewish defenders. He was so amazed by the enormity and strength of the Jewish strongholds that he declared:

> We have certainly had God for our assistant in this war, and it was no other than God that ejected the Jews out of these fortifications; for what could the hands of men, or any machines, do towards overthrowing these towers![23]

ARCH OF TITUS

The majority of Jewish survivors were rounded up and sold into abject slavery. Others were consigned to die in the gladitorial exhibitions, or were specially selected to be paraded in Titus' triumphal train in Rome. There were so many survivors sold into slavery and so few buyers that the Romans could only fetch a very low price. Over 97,000 Jews

---

22. *Ibid.*, Chp. 8:5.
23. *Ibid.*, Chp. 9:1.

were auctioned off in this manner. In Josephus' concluding comments of this tragic episode in Israel's history, he gives the statistics of the number slain and captured: "Now the number of those that were carried captive during this whole war was . . . 97,000, and the number who perished during the whole siege, 1,100,000."[24] He attributes the large number of Jews slain to the fact that, "a vast multitude had collected . . . and the Roman army encompassed the city when it was crowded with inhabitants."[25]

The "Arch of Titus" was erected in Rome to commemorate Titus' victory over Jerusalem. Sculpture upon the arch is a procession carrying the spoils plundered from the Jewish temple. The golden table, the candlestick, the veils of the sanctuary, and the Book of the Law can be seen in the relief.

Thus ended the *great tribulation* of which Jesus had prophesied. The predictions of Jerusalem's desolation were literally fulfilled. The wrath of God had been poured out as the prophets had foretold, resulting in the disbanding of the nation of Israel. Jerusalem was *trodden down of the Gentiles,* and its survivors carried captive into all the nations of the world, according to the explicit words of Christ (Luke 21:22-24). The destruction was so complete that not one stone was left standing upon another in exact accordance with the original statements of Jesus (Matthew 24:2). In fact, Josephus relates that "Caesar gave orders (after the siege) that they should now demolish the whole city and

24. *Ibid.,* Chp. 9:3.
25. *Ibid.,* Chp. 9:4.

temple . . . (and) it was laid so completely even with the ground, by those who dug it up to the foundation that there was nothing to make those that came thither believe it had ever been inhabited."[26]

The unparalleled tribulation of those days aptly fulfilled the words of Jesus when He predicted that: "There shall be great distress in the land, and wrath upon this people" (Luke 21:23). Not only did the Jewish nation suffer the remorseless fury of the Roman army, but they endured the unimaginable horrors of famine, pestilence, cannibalism, and the fratricidal atrocities of the seditious factions.

The accompanying illustration is of a bronze coin which was struck to commemorate the capture of Jerusalem and Judea. The front side pictures Titus and gives his titles in abbreviated Latin. The reverse side is inscribed "Judea Capta" - "Captive Judea." A Jewish woman is seen weeping to the left of the palm tree; on the opposite side a Jewish man stands with hands tied behind his back.

The remnant that survived faced the further humiliations of being sold into slavery and being dispersed throughout the earth. Josephus noted that the afflictions which befell the Jews were,

the greatest of all those, not only that have been in our times, but, in a manner, of those wherein cities have fought against cities, or nations against nations . . . it appears to me that the misfortunes of all men, from the beginning of the world, if they be compared to those of the Jews, are not so considerable as they were.[27]

How accurate were the prophetic words which said, "And they shall fall by the edge of the sword, and shall be led away captive into all nations" (Luke 21:24a).

---

26. *Ibid.*, Bk. 7, Chp. 1.
27. Flavius Josephus, *Preface to Wars*, 1 & 4, p. 427-428.

Questions for Discussion

1. Do you feel that Josephus is a reliable witness? Why?
2. Is it justified to use secular literature or records to support biblical perspectives? Can you find any biblical examples where God used the unrighteous to fulfill His purposes?
3. List any potential dangers in using secular research materials.
4. Do you agree with those who claim that Josephus' historical account of Jerusalem's destruction was providentially preserved for our instruction? Why?
5. As an assignment, read Josephus' eyewitness account of the Jewish uprising. This is covered in Josephus' "Wars of the Jews," Book 2, chapter 1, through Book 6, chapter 10.
6. Discuss how that generation of Jews had brought the cup of God's wrath to full brim.
7. Do you see any prophetic parallels between the warnings of Moses in Deuteronomy 28:15-68, and the historic events of 70 A.D.? Is it justified to link Moses' prophetic statements with 70 A.D.?

"THROUGH MUCH TRIBULATION"

Chapter Twelve

"THROUGH MUCH TRIBULATION"

Nowhere in the scriptures does the word "tribulation" refer to a final, seven year period of unparalleled distress at the close of this present age. Though dispensationalists apply the term "great tribulation" to a strict futuristic setting, the scripture references using the word *tribulation* clearly refute this teaching.

Thlipsis

The Greek word for tribulation is "thlipsis." It is used numerous times in the New Testament, and is translated in a variety of ways. It is used four times in referring to the judgments which befell the Jews in 70 A.D., three times in reference to the punishments which are inflicted upon the wicked, and thirty-seven times in reference to the general tribulations afflicting God's people. However, it is never used in connection with a final period of turmoil at the end of this age.

Jesus employed the word "thlipsis" in Matthew 24:21 when referring to the "great TRIBULATION (thlipsis)." In Mark, the same word is translated *affliction* in the phrase, "for in those days shall be AFFLICTION (thlipsis)" (Mark 13:19). Though Luke's companion account does not include the word tribulation, he characterizes the same period as "the days of vengeance," "distress," and "wrath upon the people" (Luke 21:22, 23). As we have seen, it is clear from the context of these parallel passages that they are each referring to the selfsame judgments which overtook the Jewish nation in 70 A.D.

A further proof that Christ's reference to the "great tribulation" was fulfilled in 70 A.D. is demonstrated by the fact

112

that after stating that such suffering had not been witnessed since the beginning of the world, He continued by stressing, "no, nor ever shall be" (Matthew 24:21; Mark 13:19). This statement would have been pointless if this tribulation period was to occur at the close of this age, for then there would be no remaining time to prove this point.

"In the World Ye Shall Have Tribulation"

A study of the word "thlipsis" proves that tribulation is no stranger to God's people. In varying degrees, it has been the common denominator of all ages. In a variety of forms, it has been the plight of all believers. There is nothing in the statements of Christ or the apostles to support the belief that Christianity has been granted immunity from tribulations. Even a cursory glance of church history reveals that the gospel age has been marked by repetitious tribulations for Christians. When we consider the millions who were butchered by the Roman emperors, martyred by the Catholic Inquisitions, tortured, imprisoned, and banished, we recognize in a far broader sense that this entire age has been one of incredible tribulation for God's people.

There isn't a single New Testament passage which suggests that Christ has granted us exemption from tribulations. At the very threshold of this age, Jesus affirmed that the Christian life was not one of ease, but one of tribulation: "These things I have spoken unto you, that in me ye might have peace. In the world YE SHALL HAVE TRIBULATION: but be of good cheer; I have overcome the world" (John 16:33).

Paul also informed the church that,

113

. . . we must through MUCH TRIBULATION enter into
the kingdom of God (Acts 14:22).

He also reminded us that:

. . . we SHOULD SUFFER TRIBULATION (I Thessalonians
3:4).

The Greek word *thlipsis* is repeatedly used in reference to
the common lot of sufferings which Christians endure in the
course of ordinary life, and our response to them (Romans
5:3; 8:35; 12:12; II Corinthians 1:4; 2:4; 7:4; Ephesians
3:13; I Thessalonians 3:4; II Thessalonians 1:4).

"Affliction"

The word thlipsis is frequently translated *affliction*. Early
in the Olivet prophecy, Jesus stated that believers would
be delivered up "to be AFFLICTED" (Matthew 24:9). In
the parable of "the seed and the sower," Jesus referred to
those who would be offended when afflictions arose (Mark
4:7; see also Matthew 13:21).

In Acts 20:23, Paul spoke of his "bonds and AFFLIC-
TIONS." He wrote to the Corinthians "out of much AFFLIC-
TION and anguish of heart" (II Corinthians 2:4). In II Corinthians 4:17; he revealed that "our light AFFLICTIONS
are but for a moment." He talked about "approving ourselves as the ministers of God, in much patience, in AFFLIC-
TIONS. . . ." (II Corinthians 6:4). He referred to the "great
trial of AFFLICTIONS" the Macedonian churches endured
(II Corinthians 8:2). In Philippians 1:15, he chided those
who sought to add to his afflictions, and then followed by
thanking the Philippian church for ministering to him in
his affliction (Philippians 4:14). He spoke of filling up that

114

which is behind of the "AFFLICTIONS of Christ" in his flesh (Colossians 1:24). He commended the Thessalonians for receiving the word in "much AFFLICTION" (I Thessalonians 1:6), and exhorted them that "no man should be moved by the AFFLICTIONS; for yourselves know that we are appointed thereunto" (I Thessalonians 3:3). In I Thessalonians 3:7, Paul spoke of being comforted ". . . in all our AFFLICTIONS." And finally, Paul referred to the "reproaches and AFFLICTIONS" which the Jewish Christians endured (Hebrews 10:33).

The word *thlipsis* is also translated "trouble" in II Corinthians 1:8 when Paul mentions the ". . . TROUBLE which came to us in Asia . . . insomuch that we despaired of life." It is also used in reference to the "PERSECUTION that arose about Stephen" (Acts 11:19). It is also found in a number of verses which have absolutely nothing to do with the *great tribulation* ("anguish," John 16:21; "affliction," Acts 7:10, 11; "trouble," I Corinthians 7:28; and "burdened," II Corinthians 8:13).

Tribulation Upon the Wicked

The word *thlipsis* is also used in connection with the judgments which will come upon the ungodly at the end of the world. In referring to "the day of wrath and revelation of the righteous judgment of God," the Word speaks of those who will receive ". . . wrath, TRIBULATION, and anguish" (Romans 2:5-9). In II Thessalonians 1:6, we read that "it is a righteous thing with God to recompense TRIBULATION" to the wicked. Paul reveals that this will occur when "the Lord Jesus shall be revealed from heaven with his mighty angels, in flaming fire, taking vengeance on them

115

that know not God" (verse 7), and not during a prolonged period of wrath which dispensationalists refer to as the "Great Tribulation."

The "Great Tribulation" of Revelation 7:14

It would be pertinent at this juncture of study to briefly comment upon the only other verses in the Bible which specifically mention a period of "great tribulation." I do this because of their verbal correspondence to Matthew 24:21. Both of these verses are found in the book of Revelation. Though the word tribulation (thlipsis) occurs five times in the book of Revelation, only two of these passages (Revelation 2:22; 7:14) have any bearing upon the subject of the great tribulation.

Three of these verses (Revelation 1:9; 2:9, 10) are addressed to Christians, and simply refer to events in this life. When writing to the seven churches of Asia, John referred to himself as "your brother and companion in TRIBULATION" (Revelation 1:9). The letter to the church at Smyrna speaks of their "works, and TRIBULATION, and poverty" and admonishes them to "fear none of those things which thou shalt suffer . . . ye shall have TRIBULATION ten days" (Revelation 2:9, 10). However, none of these references has anything to do with a period of Great Tribulation.

The two remaining passages in Revelation do specifically refer to a great tribulation. In the letter to the church of Thyatira, Jesus warns some who were being seduced by the prophetess Jezebel, and warns them:

> Behold, I will cast her into a bed, and them that commit adultery with her into GREAT TRIBULATION, except they repent (Revelation 2:22).

116

In John's vision of the redeemed multitudes, we read:

> . . . and he said unto me, these are they which came out of GREAT TRIBULATION, and have washed their robes, and made them white in the blood of the Lamb (Revelation 7:14).

Of these two passages, only the latter has any possible bearing upon a final period of *great tribulation*. Even dispensationalists agree that the reference to *great tribulation* in Revelation 2:22 has nothing to do with a seven year period of intense travail at the close of this age.

But, does Revelation 7:14 support the Great Tribulation theory? Some are quick to point out that the original Greek text includes the article *the* in front of the phrase "great tribulation"—"THE great tribulation." But this argument is not conclusive. It does not prove a seven year tribulation period at the close of this dispensation. The Greek text also includes the article *the* in Revelation 1:9 when John was simply referring to the tribulation he was partaking of during his lifetime: "I your brother, and partaker with you in THE tribulation. . . ."

The adjective *great* in "great tribulation" requires some qualification. The word can be viewed extensively, as well as intensively. It can apply to either an extended period of suffering involving an indefinite length of time, or to a brief period of intense distress. Dispensationalists assign it wholly to a future period of unprecedented suffering lasting for seven (or 3-1/2) years. However, it seems arbitrary to restrict its application to an almost negligible period of time at the end of this age when we consider the intense and prolonged tribulation which the church has already endured.

Many consign the phrase *great tribulation* to a strict, end-time setting. This is commonly done with the phrase "great

117

tribulation" found in Matthew 24:21 and Revelation 7:14. However, there is no evidence which distinctly links these parallel statements to the same historical event or time frame. The *great tribulation* of Matthew's account was an obvious episode of past history, which strictly applied to the Jewish nation of Palestine in 66-70 A.D., while the *great tribulation* of Revelation 7:14 is more general in nature, indefinite in scope, involving people out of every nation, kindred, tongue, and tribe. There is absolutely no internal or external justification in the passages from Revelation for anyone to restrict the expression *great tribulation* to a definite end-time scenario.

The precise timing of this period is not indicated in the slightest, except by reading into this expression our own prophetic perspectives and timetables. Neither is there any information given to support the common dispensationalist term of "tribulation saints" (meaning a unique company of believers who will supposedly live and die during an end-time period of tribulation). The wording, "these are they which came out of great tribulation" does not refer to a special class of afflicted saints differing from all other saints of the church age who have also been called upon to suffer tribulation. There is nothing in the context or usage of this expression to limit its application to a body of believers who will weather a unique period of end-time tribulation. It is simply a general reference to the believers of all ages who have suffered for the truth's sake. This verse applies to all Christians who have passed through the afflictions characteristic of the entire breadth of the church age. The group mentioned in verses 9-17 clearly refers to the departed dead in heaven who have endured the tribulation of this age.

There is no valid scriptural defense for the teaching of a separate company of *tribulation* saints segregated from the main body of the redeemed. This concept is purely aribtrary. To limit this term to a select company of Christians at the end of this age, when the entire body of Christendom has suffered the pangs of countless tribulations, is an insult to the millions who have laid down their lives for Christ. To maintain that the martyrs of nearly two millennia have not been included among these saints seems inconceivable. It is an idea which is not supported by scriptural evidence.

In concluding our study on the word *tribulation*, we have seen that it has a variety of applications. Though it is used over forty times in the New Testament, not a single reference lends itself to a seven year period of tribulation. When taken in context and viewed as a whole, we discover that the usage of the word *tribulation* does not support the futuristic concept of a brief period of intense tribulation at the close of this age. Instead, the word represents tribulation as one of the distinguishing features of this entire dispensation.

Questions for Discussion

1. As a project, review the usage of the word *thlipsis* (*Strongs*, 2347) in the New Testament.
2. Does the prosperous church of America suffer tribulation? Is tribulation always in the form of physical suffering? Please explain.
3. Can you find any scripture passages which clearly teach that Christians would escape a great tribulation period through a pre-tribulation rapture.

4. Discuss why God has appointed us to go through tribulations (I Thessalonians 3:3, 4).
5. Do you think the Christians which endured the persecutions of the Roman emperors, the Spanish inquisitions, or the threat of Mohammedism could have found justifiable reasons for believing that they were passing through great tribulation? Has this ever been the historical case?

"THE TIMES OF THE GENTILES"

Chapter Thirteen

"THE TIMES OF THE GENTILES"

MATT. 24	MARK 13	LUKE 21
		24 And they shall fall by the edge of the sword, and shall be led away captive into all nations: and Jerusalem shall be trodden down of the Gentiles, until the times of Gentiles be fulfilled.

The nation of Israel had tasted the bitter cup of God's wrath. The kingdom had been wrenched from her possession and given to others. What would now become of Israel in the aftermath of those tragic "days of vengeance"? Did the great tribulation mark the terminal point of God's dealings with the Jewish peoples? Had He washed His hands of them forever? Now that the nation had been disbanded and its surviving remnant scattered throughout the earth, what prospects of hope, if any, did the future hold?

In the context of referring to those awesome days of affliction, Jesus had revealed that the Jewish nation would "fall by the edge of the sword and be led away captive into all nations" (Luke 21:24). He then followed with the cryptic revelation that Jerusalem would be "trodden down by the Gentiles until the time of the Gentiles be fulfilled." The meaning of this puzzling phrase has been the repeated grounds of uncertainty for many an expositor. The enigmatic expression "the times of the Gentiles" is found only in Luke's Olivet account, and a variety of explanations have been suggested in an attempt to unravel its inherent mystery.

By Implication

This phrase follows immediately upon the heels of Christ's comments concerning the divinely orchestrated judgments which befell the Jewish nation in 66-70 A.D. The manner in which this expression is employed in conjunction with the outpouring of God's wrath upon the Jews, coupled with the emphasis upon the *Gentiles* in relationship to that catastrophic event, suggests three important things:

1. During this extended period of God's displeasure, a definite dispensation of grace has been allotted to the Gentile nations in God's sovereign dealings to the exclusion of the Jews. The predominate emphasis during this dispensation would be upon the Gentiles, as evidenced by the phrase "times of the Gentiles."

2. The wrath of God (see Luke 21:23), which was initially unleashed upon that nation and the city of Jerusalem at the hands of the Gentile powers, was only the beginning of a lengthy period of distress which would afflict the Jews, as evidenced by the statement: "And Jerusalem shall be trodden down of the Gentiles until the times of the Gentiles be fulfilled."

3. However, in spite of the Jews' past failures, their future destiny has a distinctly positive outlook, as evidenced by the fact that the "times of the Gentiles" are stated to have established limits (be fulfilled) and by the companion statements of the Apostle Paul (Romans 11) concerning the future prospects of the Jewish people.

Stripped of Privilege

It was due to Israel's corporate rebellion and obstinate refusal to embrace Christ as their Messiah that God initially poured out His vengeance upon the Jewish nation in 70 A.D. This event marked the commencement of the overspreading of God's wrath towards the Jewish race, which was to

123

follow them into their worldwide dispersion. Because of their stubborn unwillingness to respond to God, Israel was severely punished. She then, subsequently, lost her favored status before God. The nation of Israel was stripped of her privileged position and removed from the forefront of God's dealings in the earth. In the wake of this loss of preeminence, the Gentile nations were thrust into the spotlight of God's merciful favor. During this period, the Gentiles would partake of the privileges hitherto belonging exclusively to Israel.

This historic fact is in keeping with Christ's warnings to the Jewish nation concerning the eventual excision of the unbelieving majority of the Jews and the inclusion of the Gentile peoples into the kingdom of God:

> And I say unto you, That many shall come from the east and west, and shall sit down with Abraham, and Isaac, and Jacob, in the kingdom of heaven. But the children of the kingdom shall be cast out into outer darkness: there shall be weeping and gnashing of teeth (Matthew 8:11, 12; see also Luke 13:28, 29).

In the "parable of the vineyard," we observe Christ's prediction of Israel's eventual rejection and the ensuing acceptance of the Gentiles (see Matthew 21:33-43). This parable characterizes the historic rebellion of the Jewish peoples towards the messengers of God culminating in the murder of God's own Son. Through parabolic imagery Jesus forewarns the Jews of their impending judgment and the resulting forfeiture of their privileged standing before God:

> He will miserably destroy those wicked men (Jewish nation) and will let out his vineyard (kingdom of God) unto other husbandmen (Gentiles), which shall render him the fruits in their seasons (Matthew 21:41).

And again in verse 43 we read:

> Therefore say I [Jesus] unto you [Jews], The kingdom of God
> shall be taken from you, and given to a nation [spiritual
> Israel comprised mainly of Gentile believers] bringing forth
> the fruits thereof.

In the "parable of the marriage of the king's son," Jesus
re-emphasized these truths:

> The kingdom of heaven is like unto a certain king, which
> made a marriage for his son, and sent forth his servants to
> call them that were bidden to the wedding: and they would
> not come. . . . But they made light of it, and went their ways,
> one to his farm, another to his merchandise: and the rem-
> nant took his servants, and entreated them spitefully, and
> slew them. *But when the king heard thereof, he was wroth:
> and he sent forth his armies, and destroyed those murderers,
> and burned up their city* (Matthew 22:2-7).

It should be noted that this parable prophetically forewarns
the Jews of Jerusalem's impending desolation (verse 7).

The historic proof that God did indeed shift the focus of
His attention towards the Gentiles can also be observed in
the declarations of the Apostle Paul (see Acts 13:46, 47;
28:25-28).

A Protracted Period of Disfavor

As a direct result of Israel's corporate decision to spurn
the gospel, the Gentiles became the principle recipients of
God's merciful overtures for an allotted period of time. Not
only did God shift the essential thrust of His dealings away
from natural Israel, but He also employed the Gentiles as
a vehicle to execute His judgment against the Jewish nation
in 70 A.D.

The fact that Jesus carefully informed His disciples that Jerusalem would be trodden down until the "times of the Gentiles" were fulfilled, reveals to us that Israel was destined to endure a protracted period of God's disfavor beginning with the desolation of Jerusalem in 70 A.D. The phrase "trodden down of the Gentiles" was meant to denote something more than mere domination and Gentile subjugation of Jerusalem. It indicated the indignity, disgrace, and humiliation which the entire Jewish race would bear because of their rebellion against the purposes of God in the earth.

When Jesus stated that Jerusalem would be "trodden down" by Gentile powers, He was not singularly intending to convey the idea that the literal city of Jerusalem would be subjugated by Gentiles for an indeterminate period, though His statement could include this aspect; but, in a far broader sense, He was informing His followers that the devastating wrath which initially visited the Jews in 70 A.D. marked only the beginning of a lengthy period of God's lingering displeasure towards the Jewish people. For an indeterminate, yet distinct interval of time, Jerusalem (which was used as a geographical symbol to represent the entire Jewish national existence) will endure the extended distresses of God's punishments toward them. This has been the undeniable, historic plight of the Jews throughout the intervening centuries.

A Hopeful Prospect?

Though the Jewish race was destined to remain under this prolonged dispensation of God's disfavor, Jesus clearly stated that the times of the Gentiles will eventually reach their limits. Though it is the current belief of some that

126

Israel's judgment is irrevocable and any hope for reconciliation impossible, the scriptures clearly imply the opposite. If we carefully weigh the key statements of Paul concerning the future destiny of the Jews, we can readily see that they yet await the glorious prospect of inclusion into the family of God "on a scale not hitherto witnessed."[1] Though some have doctrinally "cast off" Israel, Paul's revelations concerning the fate of Jewry clearly challenges this assumption.

Even Christ Himself had included a hopeful word concerning the eventual fate of the Jewish peoples in His final comments to the ecclesiastical authorities. In consummating His withering denunciation against them, He had stated that their house would be left desolate until such a time as the Jews would say:

> Blessed is he that cometh in the name of the Lord (Matthew 23:39).

His words clearly imply that the day would come when the Jews would respond to the Messiah they once rejected.

A balanced perspective of the future destiny of the Jewish race is impossible, apart from a careful examination of the crucial truths contained within Romans chapter 11. Regarding this chapter, Mauro noted: "It contains a strong intimation that it lay in the purpose of God, at some time in the then future, to extend special mercy to the Jews (Romans 11:24, 26, 31)."[2]

In reference to the Jews' future standing before God, Paul questions whether their present condition of disfavor and exclusion is absolute:

> Hath God cast away his people (Jews)? (Romans 11:1a).

---

1. Philip Mauro, *The Hope of Israel*, pp. 151-152.
2. *Ibid.*, p. 170.

In other words, are we correct in presuming that God's rejection of Israel is complete and unconditional? Paul's immediate reply is emphatic:

GOD FORBID! (Romans 11:1).

Though only a small remnant of Jewry has accepted Christ and entered the election according to grace (spiritual Israel), their overwhelming historic response has been one of obstinacy and spiritual blindness (Romans 11:7, 8). Paul, however, rejects the assumption that their fall is permanent, absolute, and irrevocable. In verse 11, he inquires, "Have they stumbled that they should fall?" In other words, he asks if they are irretrievably lost—whether their estrangement is permanent. Again he replies, "God forbid!" His statement implies that their rejection is only temporary.

What is more, he follows with the glorious revelation that as a direct result of their temporary state of defection, God has extended the riches of His grace to the Gentile nations in their place; and this, in turn, will eventually work to provoke the Jewish people to envy when they witness the goodness of God poured out upon the Gentiles (Romans 11:11).

In verse 15, Paul states:

For if the casting away of them be the reconciling of the world, what shall the receiving of them be, but life from the dead? (Romans 11:15).

His obvious implication is that natural Israel will ultimately experience a reconciliation with God as evidenced by the phrase, "what shall the receiving of them be, but life from the dead?" As Mauro noted: "The words 'receiving of them,' following the words 'the casting away of them,' indicate that

128

Paul was not without hope that numbers of Jews might yet be saved."[3]

"Grafted In"

Paul employs the figure of the olive tree to illustrate what God's salvation does for Jews and Gentiles alike. In verse 20, Paul states that "because of unbelief they (Jews) were broken off" and adds that "they also, if they abide not still in unbelief, shall be grafted in" (verse 23). His words carry an air of hopefulness concerning the distinct possibility of Israel's eventual inclusion into the olive tree.

Mauro's comments upon this illustration are helpful:

Paul is here speaking of the salvation—not merely of an occasional individual, but of that great mass of the people, represented by the branches broken off from the olive tree. Thus, while the passage intimates, on the one hand, that there may come a time when the Jews as a whole will be much more receptive of the message of the gospel than they have been during the centuries past, it makes it plain . . . that the only salvation for them is the same olive tree salvation whereof Gentiles who believe in Jesus Christ are made partakers, and that the condition of their being saved is that 'they continue not in unbelief.' "[4]

"Their Fulness"

Paul further addresses the prospects of Israel's eventual inclusion into the church of God by stating:

---

3. *Ibid.*, p. 148.
4. *Ibid.*, p. 149.

> Now if the fall of them be the riches of the world, and the diminishing of them the riches of the Gentiles, how much more their FULNESS? (Romans 11:12).

The obvious implication of this verse is that though Israel has entered a period of *diminishing,* the time will arrive when she will experience her *fulness.*

He inserts the enlightening admonition concerning the Gentile relationship to this inevitable *fulness:*

> For I would not, brethren, that ye should be ignorant of this mystery, lest ye should be wise in your own conceits; that blindness in part is happened to Israel, UNTIL THE FULNESS OF THE GENTILES BE COME IN (Romans 11:25).

This important verse is directly related to the phrase, "the times of the Gentiles be fulfilled" in Luke 21:24. In this passage, the companion expression, "until the fulness of the Gentiles be come in" is employed. It should be noted that the words *fulfilled* (Luke 21:24), and *fulness* (Romans 11:12, 25) are derived from the same Greek word (*pleroo*). At the season of the Gentiles' fulness ("the times of the Gentiles"), Israel will begin to experience a corresponding season of fulness. As Matthew Henry wrote:

> When the fulness of the Gentiles shall come in, when the gospel shall have had its intended success and made its progress in the Gentile world . . . all Israel shall be saved. Not every individual person, but the body of the people. Not that they should ever be restored to their covenant of peculiarity again, to have their priesthood and temple, and ceremonies again, but they shall be brought into belief in the Messiah and be incorporated in the Christian church.[5]

---

5. Matthew Henry, *Matthew Henry's Commentary, Vol. 5.*

Philip Mauro's comments on Romans 11:25 are worthy of consideration:

> All this being understood, it yet remains that the passage in Romans 11:25 leaves room for, even if it does not imply, a time to come during this gospel era when the supernatural blindness, imposed as a punishment upon the Jews as a nation, will be removed, or at least abated, so that the gospel message will have a far greater effect among them than during the time the veil was upon their hearts, and that many of them may be saved. Paul's heart's desire and prayer to God for Israel was "that they might be saved"; and it is reasonable to assume that, in so praying, he was "praying in the Holy Ghost." This lends support to the expectation that there will yet be a mighty working of the Spirit and the Word of God amongst the Jewish people, something analogous to "the latter rain"—in which, of course, Gentiles too will participate.[6]

A Clarification

I should clarify any misconceptions that I am implying that every Jew will eventually be saved, or that even a majority of the Jewish race will awaken from their spiritual stupor. But the degree of receptivity and the proportion of those who will respond to the gospel will surpass anything previously witnessed during the times of the Gentiles.

I should further stress that this prospect of Jewish responsiveness to the gospel lends absolutely no support to the popular dispensationalist teaching of a total national restoration of Israel in a separate and distinct dispensation of God. It gives no support to the implication that there will

---

6. Philip Mauro, *The Hope of Israel*, p. 147.

be another exclusive economy of salvation apart from the present gospel age. There will be no "special" post-gospel salvation for the Jews. "The promised mercy will take the form not of a special national salvation after this day of grace shall have ended."[7] The Bible knows of only one common salvation (Romans 1:16) extended to all races and capacities of men. The Jews must enter the "election of grace" on the same footing as their Gentile counterparts. There is no other hope for the Jew, past, present, or future, apart from that which is presently in effect. There are no second chances apart from "the righteousness of God which is by faith of Jesus Christ unto all and upon all them that believe: for there is no difference" (Romans 3:22).

Furthermore, when the "fulness of the Gentiles" comes in, God will not abruptly terminate His dealings with the nations, suddenly abandon the Gentiles, or completely shift His attention away from them. Instead, through the instrumentality of the predominantly Gentile church, He will reach out to the estranged nation of Jewry. Paul strongly implies that the church of Jesus Christ, comprised mainly of Gentile believers, will be the principle instrument used to promote this Jewish reconciliation:

> For as ye in times past have not believed God, yet have now obtained mercy through their unbelief: even so have these also now not believed, THAT THROUGH YOUR MERCY THEY ALSO MAY OBTAIN MERCY (Romans 11:30, 31).

With these brief thoughts in mind, I hold that the phrase "the times of the Gentiles be fulfilled" (Luke 21:24) is synonymous with Paul's statements concerning the "fulness of of the Gentiles" (Romans 11:25) and directly corresponds

---

7. *Ibid.*, p. 170.

to the timing of the *fulness* which the Jews are destined to experience (Romans 11:12). The world yet awaits a season, of longer or shorter duration, when the Jews will experience a greater awakening towards Christ. The predominantly Gentile church will be a key catalyst in this process of reconciliation, and the conclusion of the matter for the Jew will not be one of disappointment, but one of the ultimate blessing and *fulness* when both Jew and Gentile are incorporated into the "Israel of God"—the church of Jesus Christ.

Questions for Discussion

1. In I Thessalonians 2:16, Paul states that God's wrath is come upon them "to the uttermost." Was this statement fulfilled in 70 A.D., or is it still being fulfilled today? Please explain.
2. In light of Paul's category of sins against the Jewish people, is there valid hope for their restoration according to the scriptures? If so, explain what their inclusion must be based upon.
3. What were the divine implications of the temple's destruction and demolition of Jerusalem from the Jewish point of view.
4. Apart from the physical torments suffered by the Jews, discuss the moral and religious aspects of their punishments and sufferings.
5. Jesus stated that Jerusalem would be trodden down until the "times of the Gentiles be fulfilled." How has this been fulfilled through history? Is it still being fulfilled?
6. How have the Gentile nations replaced Israel in relationship to God's purpose in the earth?

133

7. The Jews were given great blessings and privileges—with it came awesome responsibility and accountability. What lesson should this have for the church today?

8. Are there any indications that this period of punishment is coming to an end? According to Moses' warnings in Deuteronomy 28, what were God's conditions for restoration?

9. If the Jewish people will eventually experience a time of unprecedented responsiveness to Christ, will it just affect the Jews of Palestine? What will be the principal agent—the Gentile church, or a sovereign act of God?

10. Will a Jewish responsiveness to the gospel be a definite sign of the end? Please explain.

"EXCEPT THOSE DAYS BE SHORTENED"

Chapter Fourteen

"EXCEPT THOSE DAYS BE SHORTENED"

MATT. 24	MARK 13	LUKE 21
22 And except those days should be shortened, there should no flesh be saved: but for the elect's sake those days shall be shortened.	20 And except that the Lord had shortened those days, no flesh should be saved: but for the elect's sake, whom he hath chosen, he hath shortened the days.	

So devastating would be the unprecedented tribulations attending those days, that had it not been for the restraining power of God, no flesh would have survived. As Edersheim noted: "So dreadful would be the persecution that, if Divine mercy had not interposed for the sake of the followers of Christ, the whole Jewish race that inhabited the land would have been swept away."[1] God purposefully limited the duration of those unparalleled days of distress in order to spare His elect from perishing.

The Elect?

Controversy has surrounded the specific application of the word *elect*. Some hold that it is a direct reference to the Jewish inhabitants of Palestine, while others apply it strictly to the Christian community. It would be confusing to apply the term to both the Jews upon whom God was pouring out His wrath, and to the Christians whom He was mercifully taking such painstaking measures to deliver from the holocaust. However, in taking the verse as a whole, I believe that it contains sufficient support to defend both perspectives.

Firstly, Jesus informs His disciples that had those days not been cut short, no flesh would be saved. I hold that

---

1. Alfred Edersheim, The Life and Times of Jesus the Messiah, p. 449.

this is an obvious reference to the Jews who would bear the lethal brunt of God's vengeance. Unless God had imposed limits to their sufferings, the entire population of Judea would have been annihilated. As it was, only a small remnant survived the indiscriminate slaughter perpetrated by the Roman legions and by the self-inflicted atrocities. Jesus was not exaggerating when He spoke of "no flesh being saved" as a result of the calamities of those days. One has only to review the detailed accounts of Josephus to recognize that the entire population was nearly annihilated during the siege, and no part of Judea was exempt from the terrors which befell the inhabitants of the capitol city.

The second half of this passage contains a direct reference to the Christian community dwelling in Palestine during those awesome days of the Jewish revolt (66-70 A.D.). The word *elect* (signifying the picked-out or chosen of God) is a reference to the people of God—"the election of grace" and not to the national election of Israel according to the flesh. The obvious application of this word to the Christians can be readily observed by its contextual usage in other passages of the Olivet discourse; for example, in Matthew 24:24 we read:

> For there shall arise false Christs, and false prophets, and shall shew great signs and wonders; insomuch that, if it were possible, they shall deceive the very ELECT.

The word *elect* is an undeniable reference to the body of Christ who were being warned of the appearance of false messiah during the Jewish revolt.

The Contributing Factors

Though the elect were provided detailed instructions in order to facilitate their escape, had those days of tribulation not been cut short, they too could have easily perished from lack of proper shelter, provisions, or the ever-widening fury of the Roman sword. Those days were cut short by the divisions and fratricidal slaughter within the city, the determination of the Roman legions, the famine, and the direct intervention of God. Furthermore, several other pertinent factors contributed to shortening the duration of the siege: Titus was personally disposed to clemency and moderation towards the Jews, being in love with Agrippa's sister Bernice, as well as possessing great esteem towards Josephus the historian; Vespasian's attention had increasingly turned to Rome as the prospects of emperorship brightened; an outbreak of revolts on the northern frontiers of the Empire demanded immediate attention; and Titus, who had been left in charge of the Roman forces in Judea by Vespasian, was eager to return to Rome to share in the inaugural festivities of his father. The total duration of the final siege on Jerusalem lasted less than five months, from April to September of 70 A.D.

That those days were shortened by the divine intervention of God can be attested to by the unexpected manner in which the Jewish strongholds were suddenly abandoned. So impregnable were these fortifications that had the zealots maintained their positions, they could have easily delayed the termination of the siege on Jerusalem indefinitely. In regards to this amazing withdrawal of Jewish forces from their strongholds, Josephus commented:

> They did wholly deprive themselves of the security they had in their own power, and came down from those very towers of their own accord, wherein they could never have been taken by force. . . . They left those towers of themselves; or rather *they were ejected out of them by God Himself.* . . .

The Romans, when they had gotten on the last wall without any bloodshed, could hardly believe what they found to be true.[2]

Titus himself confessed that, "We have certainly had God for our assistant in this war, and it was no other than God that ejected the Jews out of their fortifications; for what could the hands of men, or any machines, do towards over-throwing these towers!"[3]

Questions for Discussion

1. Why did God restrain His wrath against Israel? In light of Israel's persistent rebellion against God, why did He place limits on their total annihiliation? What was His purpose in sparing a remnant?
2. Are dispensationalists justified in applying the term "elect" in this passage to the Jews? How is the word *elect* used in the New Testament? Is it predominantly applied to the church or Israel? Does the New Testament usage of the term "elect" tend to support the dispensationalist perspective or not? Please explain.
3. In the process of pouring out His awesome wrath upon the nation of Israel, God purposely cut short His judgments for the sake of the church. What important lesson does this provide us?
4. Give four reasons why the siege was shortened and one example of divine intervention.

---

2. Flavius Josephus, *Wars*, Bk. 6, Chp. 8:4, 5.
3. *Ibid.*, Chp. 9:1.

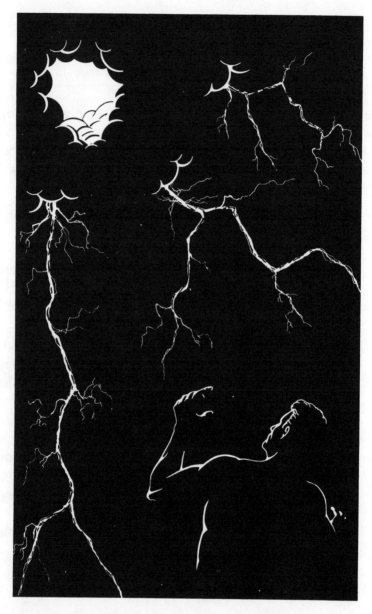

"BEHOLD, I HAVE TOLD YOU BEFORE"

Chapter Fifteen

"BEHOLD, I HAVE TOLD YOU BEFORE"

MATT. 24	MARK 13	LUKE 21
23 Then if any man shall say unto you, Lo, here is Christ, or there; believe it not.	21 And then if any man shall say to you, Lo, here is Christ; or, lo, *he is* there; believe *him* not:	
24 For there shall arise false Christs, and false prophets, and shall shew great signs and wonders; insomuch that, if *it were* possible they shall deceive the very elect.	22 For false Christs and false prophets shall rise, and shall shew signs and wonders, to seduce, if *it were* possible, even the elect.	
25 Behold, I have told you before.	23 But take ye heed: behold, I have foretold you all things.	
26 Wherefore if they shall say unto you, Behold, he is in the desert; go not forth: behold, *he is* in the secret chamber; believe *it* or not.		
27 For as the lightning cometh out of the east, and shineth even unto the west; so shall also the coming of the Son of man be.		

So lethal was the potential influence of the coming false messiahs that Jesus purposely endeavored to re-emphasize His earlier warnings concerning the pseudo-Christs who would arise in conjunction with the distresses of those days, promising deliverance to all those who co-operated with their pretentious claims. He stresses the urgency of this caution by reminding them that He had already forewarned them: "BEHOLD, I HAVE TOLD YOU BEFORE" (Matthew 24:25).

He had already alerted His followers against the threat of spiritual pretenders who would arise during the period preceding Israel's destruction (Matthew 24:5, 11), but the repeated warning, at this point, was specifically directed towards cautioning the disciples to give special heed to the admonition during the period encompassing Jerusalem's destruction. He explicitly pinpoints the timing when this warning would have its principal bearing by saying THEN, that is, during Jerusalem's siege. His disciples were not to give credence to the prophetic predictions which the spiritual imposters would circulate, or be duped by their sleight-of-hand signs and wonders. They were not to rally around their false declarations of deliverance, for no Messianic crusader or Maccabean deliverer would arise to rescue the Jews from the judgment which awaited. This was not to be a time when God would perform exploits on the behalf of the Israelite nation, but a time of God's wrath upon the Jews. As Jesus had pointedly prophesied: "For these be the days of vengeance," and, "there shall be great distress in the land, and wrath upon this people" (Luke 21:22, 23).

A Natural Assumption

In view of the numerous historic interventions of God in behalf of Israel, it would be a natural assumption for the Jews to expect another miraculous deliverance when they witnessed the invading armies of Rome encircling Jerusalem. Christ was aware that these false claimants would endeavor to capitalize upon this presumptuous belief and would easily persuade the people that the Lord was on the verge of repeating that which He had done so often in Israel's past.

The Lord was carefully informing His disciples that they were not to anticipate any form of deliverance for Israel in this instance. He well knew that His people would have a natural tendency to look expectantly for Him to return and personally rescue them during the days of *great tribulation*. He recognized the potential danger this erroneous assumption would pose for His followers. They were not to

142

entertain the rumors that the Jewish Messiah had returned and was waiting in some secluded desert location for them, or in some inner chamber in the besieged city.

Their seductive influence would be so lethal that multitudes would be drawn to their death. So real was their potential threat that the Lord stressed that "if it were possible, they shall deceive the very elect." These predictions were remarkably fulfilled during the siege on Jerusalem. Though the Christian community took to heart the urgent warnings of the Lord, untold numbers of Jews were destroyed through the promises of these religious deceivers. It is interesting to note that the Lord not only foretold the appearance of these imposters, but He also foretold the manner and circumstances of their conduct. He specified that some would claim that He was in the desert. Josephus wrote that many imposters and cheats enticed the people to follow them into the desert, promising to show them signs and wonders by the hand of God. Josephus commented upon their numbers:

> Now, as for the affairs of the Jews, they grew worse continually; for the country was again filled with robbers and imposters, who deluded the multitude. Yet did Felix catch and put to death many of those imposters every day. [1]

One such deceiver mentioned by Josephus and referred to in Acts "led out into the wilderness four thousand men, who were murderers" (Acts 21:38) claiming that, "at his command, the walls of Jerusalem would fall down."[2] Josephus also mentions another deceiver who arose in the aftermath of Jerusalem's sacking and persuaded a number to follow him into the desert, but he was captured and burned alive.[3]

---

1. Flavius Josephus, *Antiquities*, Bk. 20, Chp. 8:5, 6.
2. *Ibid.*, Chp. 8:6.
3. Flavius Josephus, *Wars*, Bk. 7, Chp. 11.

Shrouded in Secrecy?

Other false prophets claimed the manifestation of God's deliverance in connection with a secret chamber. Josephus refers to one deceiver who "made a public proclamation in the city that God commanded them to get up upon the temple, and that there they should receive miraculous signs of their deliverance."[4] About 6,000 people responded to his assurances and congregated in one of the storage rooms near the temple, but instead of deliverance, the building was torched by the Roman soldiers, and all the Jews burned to death in the inferno. Josephus added that there were then a great number of false prophets who declared to the people that they should wait for the immediate deliverance of God.

The Lord employed a simple illustration to counter the imposters' claims that the Lord had subtly appeared or that His coming would somehow be veiled in mystery. In the face of the supposed mystery and subtlety surrounding His return, Jesus forcefully asserted that His coming would be very conspicuous:

> For as the lightning cometh out of the east, and shineth even unto the west; so shall also the coming of the Son of man be (Matthew 24:27; see also Luke 17:24).

Contrary to the claims of these false prophets, Christ's advent will not be shrouded in secrecy or obscurity. It will be spectacular, patent, and universal. Christ's second coming will not only be obvious, it will be as instantaneous, unexpected, and unannounced as the flash of lightning. Though no one will foresee it, all eyes will see it. There will be no preliminary signs to indicate its manifestation.

---

4. *Ibid.*, Bk. 6, Chp. 5:2.

A Timeless Caution

Jesus was providing balance for the Christians who would be inclined to expect His immediate advent in connection with the turbulence of those days (66-70 A.D.). However, in a much larger context, He is cautioning Christians of all ages not to be swayed by deceptive teachings which claim that Christ's coming will be characterized by silence or subtlety. He flatly rejects the concept that His appearance will be somehow cloaked in secrecy. Too often in the history of the church, elements within the Christian community have been foolishly misled by either the blatant delusions of spiritual quacks, or the imbalanced and misguided instructions of good-intentioned Christians concerning the characteristics of the Lord's return. The Christian's credulity and gullibility have often been played upon by those who have implied that the Lord's return would be secret and mysterious. Periodically, history has witnessed the pathetic flocking of misdirected Christians to some lonely plain, mountaintop, or secluded house meeting to await their rendevouz with the Lord, only to be disappointed and disillusioned. Jesus was endeavoring to protect His followers from all those who would disturb the church with imbalanced perspectives and disruptive influences concerning the timing of Christ's return. The Christian community has always needed to guard itself against any prophetic persuasions which work to agitate, unsettle, or produce instability and consternation in the way we react to the subject of the Lord's return. The Apostle Paul carefully strove to correct such imbalanced tendencies among the Thessalonian believers, and his timeless admonition still applies:

> Now we beseech you, brethren, by the coming of our Lord Jesus Christ, and by our gathering together unto him, that ye be not soon shaken in mind, or be troubled, neither by

145

spirit, nor by word, nor by letter as from us as that the day of Christ is at hand (II Thessalonians 2:1, 2).

In spite of whatever the source of disruptive influences associated with the topic of the Lord's appearance, the church of Jesus Christ must always take heed not to be overcome by the adverse effects of a troubled spirit or an agitated state of mind. The Lord will return in a bold and unexpected manner; but in the meantime, the church should not be found "gazing into the heavens," chasing foolish prophetic tangents, be troubled with confusion and apprehension, or distracted from the great responsibilities entrusted to her care.

Questions for Discussion

1. In characterizing His coming, Jesus implied that it would not be subtle or mysterious, but as bold and noticeable as a flash of lightning. What impact does this revelation have upon the theory of a secret rapture?
2. Can you give any historic examples of Christians being misled by a belief in a secret return of Christ?
3. Why did Christ repeat the warning of false Christs? List all the parallel verses in the three accounts which contain warnings about spiritual imposters.
4. Does the fact that the Jews naturally assumed that God would miraculously intervene on their behalf during the siege say anything to us about the sin of presumption?
5. Can you provide any other biblical examples where false Christs offered false assurances of deliverance?
6. Mark's gospel pinpoints the time when this warning of false Christs would have its principal bearing. What time period does the word *then* in this context refer to?

"WHERESOEVER THE CARCASE IS"

Chapter Sixteen

"WHERESOEVER THE CARCASE IS"

MATT. 24	MARK 13	LUKE 21
28 For wheresoever the carcase is, there will the eagles be gathered together.		

A Principle of Judgment

What did the Lord mean by this graphic expression? Many expositors have differed over the intended application of this proverbial saying. Some have limited its application to the judgment inflicted upon Israel in 70 A.D., while others have isolated its reference strictly to Christ's return in judgment (II Thessalonians 1:6-9) at the end of this age. In actuality, both opinions contain appropriate truth, simply because the Lord was not primarily striving to locate the specific timing of this statement as much as He was endeavoring to establish a general principle concerning the judgment of God.

This unique figure of speech was clearly employed by the Lord to liken the judgment of God to the characteristic behavior of birds of prey swooping down upon a rotting carcass. The word translated "eagle" (Greek: *aetos*) in the authorized version can mean either eagle or vulture, though vultures were probably the intended meaning since eagles do not eat carrion nor gather in flocks. One writer commented upon the general application of this expression as follows: "A proverbial saying terrifically verified at the destruction of Jerusalem, and many times since, though its most tremendous illustration will be at the world's final day."[1] Another stated:

---

1. Jamieson, Fausset, Brown, *Commentary on the New Testament*, p. 327.

148

In what was probably a well-known Palestinian proverb (Jesus) points out that where there is spiritual decay, judgment will follow relentlessly and assuredly—this refers to what happens through all ages, but especially to the time of the end.[2]

Jesus was using a familiar proverb to emphasize that an event would transpire (in this instance, the judgment of God) when the required conditions were fulfilled. Specifically in the case of natural Israel, or the end of the world in general, when each had reached the necessary extremity of spiritual decay, the judgment of God would fall as swiftly and as naturally as vultures who swoop down upon a carcass.

The Carcase of Israel

This expression is closely linked to the previous passages involving the obviousness of His return, as well as the subject of false messiahs who would arise with phoney assurances of impending deliverance for the Jews. He had carefully striven to correct any misconceptions in His disciples' thinking concerning His supposed appearance to deliver His people in conjunction with Jerusalem's siege. Contrary to the false assurances which would be circulated during those days of distress, no new champion would arise to rescue Israel.

By means of this proverbial saying, the Lord figuratively characterized the awesome events which were destined to overtake the Jewish nation. Instead of satisfying their anticipated hopes for deliverance, He only forewarns them of the devastating judgments which awaited the nation. In spite of the pretentious claims of false prophets, God was not coming to deliver but to judge. The consuming wrath

---

2. Norval Geldenhuys, *Commentary on the Gospel of Luke*, p. 442.

of God would be gathered against the deserving nation as naturally and inevitably as vultures are attracted to carrion.

This dramatic figure of speech likens God's judgments to the actions of vultures who are instinctively drawn to the presence of something dead; who, when detecting it, fasten upon it and devour it. This would be an appropriate fate for the spiritually corrupt nation of Israel. As Matthew Henry commented:

> The Jews were so corrupt and degenerate, so vile and vicious, that they were become a carcass, obnoxious to the righteous judgment of God; they were also so factious and seditious, and every way so provoking to the Romans, that they had made themselves obnoxious to their resentments, and an inviting prey to them. . . . When a people (Jews) do by their sin make themselves carcasses, putrid and loathsome, nothing can be expected but that God should send eagles among them, to devour and destroy them.[3]

Many have seen in Christ's reference of eagles a direct allusion to the eagles mounted upon the ensigns which the Roman legions carried into battle. Be this as it may, God did, in effect, employ the Roman's fury as a swarm of hungry vultures to devour the rotting carcass of the Jewish nation.

In a larger sense, this proverbial expression has an ultimate application to the final judgment which will befall the world at the end of this age. The second coming of Christ is coupled with the divine summons of all the fowls of the air to flock together unto the supper of God (Revelation 19:17, 18). The context in which this parallel expression is employed in Luke 17:37 strongly suggests that it is to be placed in an end-time setting as well.

However, whether we take this proverbial expression to be a direct reference to Jerusalem's destruction in 70 A.D.,

---

3. Matthew Henry, *Matthew Henry's Commentary*, Vol. 5.

or strictly apply it to the end, the general principle of God's judgment remains unaltered. God's judgments will inevitably fall upon the deserving at the appropriate season and in His own good time.

Questions for Discussion

1. Can you list any other interpretations or applications of this verse other than the one which views it as a principle of judgment?
2. Why did Jesus intentionally employ the graphic figure of a carcass when referring to the necessary conditions for God's judgment?
3. When we consider the sins of Israel, is it justified to characterize her as a rotting carcass? Please explain.
4. What other New Testament passages mention God's judgment in conjunction with Jesus' return?
5. Should this passage be taken in a purely figurative or literal sense? Was it at least partially fulfilled with the outpouring of God's judgments in 70 A.D.?
6. This passage is also found in Luke 17:37; however, in light of its context, many view it in reference to God's coming for His body—the church. Do you feel its contextual placement in this passage justifies this interpretation? Please explain.

"SIGNS IN THE SUN, MOON, AND STARS"

Chapter Seventeen

"SIGNS IN THE SUN, MOON, AND STARS"

MATT. 24	MARK 13	LUKE 21
29 Immediately after the tribulation of those days shall the sun be darkened, and the moon shall not give her light, and the stars shall fall from heaven, and the powers of the heavens shall be shaken:	24 But in those days, after that tribulation, the sun shall be darkened, and the moon shall not give her light. 25 And the stars of heaven shall fall, and the powers that are in heaven shall be shaken.	25 And there shall be signs in the sun, and in the moon, and in the stars; and upon the earth distress of nations, with perplexity; the sea and the waves roaring; 26 Men's hearts failing them for fear, and for looking after these things which are coming on the earth: for the powers of heaven shall be shaken.

Are we nearing a day when the entire creation will be thrown into catastrophic convulsions? Will Christ's return be preceded by unprecedented cosmic phenomena? Will the celestial sphere be so jolted that stars will actually fall from heaven, the sun's glory will really be extinguished, and the moon will literally turn to blood? Is this the scenario that Christ was depicting in His reference to signs in the heavens? Was He actually describing the chaotic conditions that will one day shake the universe? These are disturbing questions which we will now address.

Signs of the End?

Thus far, the Lord had mainly concentrated on the events accompanying the destruction of Israel and the ensuing world-wide dispersion of the Jewish people. He had dwelt upon those catastrophic events which would be fulfilled before that generation passed. However, He now begins to focus upon those events which would follow in the immediate aftermath of Jerusalem's desolation.

Many apply the vivid language employed in these parallel verses to the preliminary events associated with the second

153

coming. They base their opinion upon the erroneous assumption that the "Great Tribulation" is an event at the end of the age, and because they view the mention of signs in the sun, moon, and stars in a purely literal context. However, as I have previously indicated, and as I will further elaborate upon during the course of this study, the teachings of Christ absolutely forbids us from taking celestial disturbances, natural disasters, or international calamities as premonitory signs of His coming.

In the latter half of the Olivet discourse (Matthew 24:36; 37-39; 42-44), Jesus unequivocally forbids the popular notion that there will be a universal manifestation of extraordinary signs, both in the physical universe and upon the earth itself, to clearly herald His return. One of the principal aims of Christ's prophetic instructions was to explicitly caution believers of all generations from taking calamities to be obvious foretokens of the end.

> Obviously that warning applies throughout the entire age; for if commotions of the sort mentioned by the Lord were not indications of the nearness of His coming at the beginning of the age, *they would not be indications thereof at any later period.*[1]

Moreover, the notion that there must be dramatic signs alerting the entire world of the Lord's soon return is a concept in direct conflict with Matthew 24:27, where the strong implication is that there will be no preliminary signs to herald His final return, and also with Matthew 24:36, which plainly states that no man would know the timing of the consummation of this age.

"Immediately After"

In spite of Christ's teachings concerning the uncertainty

---

1. Philip Mauro, *Seventy Weeks and the Great Tribulation,* p. 222.

surrounding the timing of His eventual return, the over-whelming consensus òf prophetic interpretations stresses exactly the opposite. Speculative end-time scenarios have commonly been extracted from these verses mentioning celestial signs and distresses upon the earth. I recognize that the wording of these passages lends itself conveniently to many of the dramatic characterizations of the events immediately connected with the last days; however, in order to do interpretive justice to the prophetic words of Jesus concerning the precise application and timing of these "signs," we must take them in the exact contextual setting in which they were presented.

In Matthew's account we read: "Immediately after the tribulation of those days . . ." (verse 29). This statement demands close attention. That the *tribulation* here mentioned is directly linked to the *great tribulation* (verse 21) which He had previously elaborated upon, is obvious. Jesus had stressed that there would be great tribulation, and that its duration would be limited. He clearly informed us that *those days* would be shortened. The parallel passages under immediate scrutiny are specifically dealing with the events scheduled to transpire "immediately after the tribulation of those days."

The appearance of these cosmic portents and earthly distresses (Luke 21:23) were set to follow the events of 70 A.D. It should be pointed out that the word translated "immediately" means precisely that. As Butler so clearly noted, "'Immediately' does not usually make room for much of a time gap—certainly not a gap of over 2000 years."[2] It is taken from the Greek word *eutheos*, and means

---

2. Paul T. Butler, *The Gospel of Luke*, p. 485.

155

"forthwith, straightway, shortly, and immediately." It does not mean after a long delay or an indefinite period of time, as some expositors are subtly implying through the prophetic timetables they present.

Mark even more explicitly establishes the distinction in timing: "But in those days after *that* tribulation . . ." (Mark 13:24). In other words, after the specific tribulation or days of affliction which Christ had just finished describing. It should be noted that "the Lord is not speaking of any distant event, but of something immediately consequent (upon the) calamities already predicted: and that must be the destruction of Jerusalem."[3]

If the references in these verses transpire at the climax of this age, as many suggest, then we must inject a forced interpretation into the distinct statement that these signs were to commence *immediately* after the tribulation which Jesus had so explicitly isolated to the destruction of Israel in 70 A.D. Furthermore, as Tasker pointed out,

> If, therefore, reference in those verses is to the final return of the Son of man in judgment, it is necessary to come to the unsatisfactory conclusion that Jesus was mistaken, for His parousia (coming) did not come immediately after the catastrophe of A.D. 70.[4]

Literal or Figurative?

In these passages, Christ indicated that in the immediate wake of the great tribulation, cosmic disturbances in the sun, moon, and stars, as well as the outbreak of distresses among the nations were slated to commence. Debate has

---

3. Adam Clarke, *Clarke's Commentary*, Vol. 5, p. 232.
4. R. V. G. Tasker, *The Gospel According to St. Matthew*, p. 225.

centered upon the issue of whether the wording in these verses is to be taken literally or figuratively. Does the mention of the sun, moon, and stars, along with the phrase "the sea and the waves roaring," have a literal application, or are they purely symbolic in nature? When viewed against the backdrop of Christ's fundamental instructions, which strictly forbids us from taking literal, cosmic portents to be the precursory signs of His return, it would be more appropriate to attach a figurative meaning to these verses.

Furthermore, it is highly inconceivable that Jesus would purposely single out only a few isolated features of this age which was slated to witness numerous significant events. I am, therefore, compelled to accept an interpretation of these words which would make them descriptive of certain distinguishing features of this entire age, rather than limiting their reference to literal signs connected solely with the closing events of this dispensation. The contextual placement of these passages, along with the points we will consider, strongly argue against literalism. "No other section of the eschatological discourse is so indebted to scriptural imagery and language."[5]

The Exact Time Frame

Thus far, I have only briefly referred to the corresponding wording in this division. Luke's account supplies us with additional information which assists us immeasurably in interpreting the exact application of Christ's prophetic statements and in establishing the specific time frame to which these passages apply. Luke mentions the predicted

---

5. William L. Lane, *The Gospel of Mark*, p. 474.

emergence of signs in the heavenly bodies, but the manner in which he introduces the subject, coupled with the immediate context in which his statements are found, assists us in ascertaining the precise meaning, application, and timing of this difficult section of the prophecy. Luke's statements involving the appearance of celestial signs are contextually sandwiched between his references to Jerusalem's destruction (Luke 21:23, 24), and Christ's second coming (Luke 21:27).

Luke does not abruptly terminate Christ's predictions with the capture of Jerusalem, but his account follows the Jewish remnant into their world-wide dispersion lasting for a prolonged and indeterminate period. His information carries us naturally into the period following immediately upon the heels of Israel's tragic demise, referred to as "the times of the Gentiles" (Luke 21:24). It is in the specific context of this extended time span of Gentile preeminence that the passages under consideration apply. The timed appearance of these celestial signs is set within the boundaries of this extended interval between the awesome events of 70 A.D., and the close of this age. It is during this lengthy time frame that:

> There shall be signs in the sun, and in the moon, and in the stars (Luke 21:25a).

Luke also adds the additional detail that:

> . . . and upon the earth distress of nations, with perplexity; the sea and the waves roaring; men's hearts failing them for fear, and for looking after those things which are coming on the earth (Luke 21:25b, 26).

His statements depict the predominant features of the church age. He uses a figurative expression to describe the perpetual agitation and instability affecting the course of nations:

158

". . . the sea and waves roaring." This figure of speech characterizes the turbulent conditions affecting the course of nations. Scripture further supports this interpretation:

> And he saith unto me, The waters which thou sawest, where the whore sitteth, are peoples, and multitudes, and nations, and tongues (Revelation 17:15; see also Isaiah 57:20).

The waters symbolically represent nations, peoples, and multitudes. Christ's statement was obviously not a passing reference to the agitated state of the earth's oceans or turbulent tidal conditions. His statement was patently symbolic.

As prophetic spectators, we are simply provided a symbolic glimpse of the constant "ebb and flow" of earthly powers churned by the opposing cross-currents of humanity. As Mauro stated: "We find good reason for concluding that the Lord is here speaking figuratively of unusual happenings in the political firmament, that is to say, the sphere of governments, or what Paul calls 'the higher powers'."[6] The fact that Luke employs this obvious figurative expression to describe the turbulent features of this age lends support to the opinion that the signs in the sun, moon, and stars are also to be interpreted in a symbolic manner.

Luke's wording depicts the turmoil characterizing the course of modern history. His words accurately portray the universal instability, confusion, and consternation gripping the hearts of humanity. His use of the word "perplexity" (Greek: *aporia*) conveys the sense of "a loss for finding the way." It depicts the uncertain groping of nations endeavoring to discover lasting solutions to the pressing problems facing mankind. It is the picture of humanity facing

---

6. Philip Mauro, *Seventy Weeks and the Great Tribulation*, p. 268.

the frustration of repeated impasse. Luke pictures the prevailing sense of anxiety and malaise plaguing each successive generation as they weather the particular distresses assailing their moment in history.

This entire age has witnessed an endless succession of calamities and chaos. There has been little respite from wars, rumors of wars, governmental instability, economic disorders, and natural calamities. Such disturbances have been one of the predominant features of this age. On this point, Morgan raised the penetrating question: "Can you find me any period since our Lord uttered this word, of which they would not be true? The signs, as He gave them, are continuous signs."[7]

Luke's apt characterization of the historic plight of humanity can not be limited to the world's state of affairs at the close of this age, for His words appropriately apply to any period of human history. Christ was simply providing a sweeping characterization of the entire history of this age. As Morgan stated: "These are not the signs of the end, they are continuous facts. 'There shall be signs,' and the language is figurative, employed to describe the condition of earthly affairs running through the period."[8]

In prophetic language, great commotions, natural disasters, and political turmoil are often depicted figuratively through the mention of cosmic disturbances. Throughout the scriptures, the sun, moon, and stars are often employed in this symbolic manner. As Edersheim noted:

What follows in Matthew 24:29, describes the history, not of the Church—far less any visible physical signs in the literal heavens—but, in prophetic imagery, the history of the hostile

7. G. Campbell Morgan, *Gospel According to Luke*, p. 238.
8. *Ibid.*, p. 238.

powers of the world, with its lessons. A constant succession of empires and dynasties would characterize politically—and it is only the political aspect with which we are here concerned—the whole period after the extinction of the Jewish state.[9]

These verses, then, symbolically depict the unsettled and turbulent state of the world powers. Henry Swete added:

In all these cases, physical phenomena are used to describe the upheaval of dynasties, or great moral and spiritual changes, and it is unnecessary to exact any other meaning from the words when they are adopted by Christ.[10]

The Old Testament prophets frequently utilized figurative imagery when depicting tumultuous times. As Clarke commented: "In prophetic language, great commotions upon earth are often represented under the notion of commotions and changes in the heavens."[11] Symbolic figures of speech often depict cataclysmic historical events.

The use of such figurative language was a distinctive feature of ancient modes of communication, and an accepted facet of speaking within the framework of sober language. For example, in Genesis 37:9, 10, Joseph dreams about the sun, moon, and stars as symbolic reprsentations of his father, mother, and brothers. These heavenly bodies are often used to indicate various realms of earthly authority. This form of speech was so natural that the dream required no interpretation.

In ancient writings, the sun, moon, and stars were repeatedly used to represent empires, states, and kings. The darkening of these celestial bodies indicated the corresponding eclipse of their power or the overthrow of the particular

9. Alfred Edersheim, *The Life and Times of Jesus the Messiah*, p. 450.
10. Henry Swete, *The Gospel According to Mark*, p. 238.
11. Adam Clarke, *Clarke's Commentary*, Vol. 5, p. 232.

realm of authority which they represented. In a similar manner, the Old Testament prophets employed these same symbols in conveying divine truths and warnings concerning the course of nations. Such figurative expressions as "the sun shall go down," "the sun shall be turned to darkness," "light darkened in the heavens," "as light in the heavens," "the moon shall not give her light," "the moon shall withdraw its light," "the moon turned into blood," "stars shall fall," "stars darkened," "dark at noonday," and "the heavens above be black" were all used symbolically to convey the idea of disaster and distresses befalling nations.

Symbolic Language and Israel

The scriptures provide numerous examples of such symbolic language. The sun, moon, and stars are used in both a positive and a negative context. In Ecclesiastes 12:1, 2, Solomon employs the phrase "while the sun, or the light, or the moon, or the stars, be not darkened" to characterize the good times of one's life. Psalms 37:6 describes in figurative language the blessings belonging to the man who trusts in the Lord: "And he shall bring forth thy righteousness as the light, and thy judgment as the noonday." This truth is echoed in other passages as well: "Then shall thy light break forth as the morning . . . then shall thy light rise in obscurity, and thy darkness be as the noonday" (Isaiah 58); "Thy sun shall no more go down; neither shall thy moon withdraw itself: for the Lord shall be thine everlasting light, and the days of thy mourning shall be ended" (Isaiah 60:20).

However, the opposite holds true as well. When a nation was iniquitous and disobedient, their condition was described symbolically in negative terms: "We wait for light, but behold obscurity; for brightness, but we walk in darkness . . .

162

we stumble at noonday as in the night" (Isaiah 59:9, 10). The prophets repeatedly warned Israel of the consequences of her persistent disobedience. Amos told them that their portion would be destruction and punishment; it would be a time of "darkness, and not light . . . even very dark, and no brightness in it" (Amos 5:18-20); "The end is come upon my people Israel . . . I will cause the sun to go down at noon, and I will darken the earth in the clear day" (Amos 8:2-9). Ezekiel had informed Israel that they were "scattered in the cloudy and dark day" (Ezekiel 34:12). The prophets warned Judah and Jerusalem of the destruction which would be inflicted upon them by the Babylonians: "I will also stretch out my hand upon Judah, and upon the inhabitants of Jerusalem . . . a day of wasteness and desolation, a day of darkness and gloominess, a day of clouds and thick darkness" (Zephaniah 1:4, 15). Isaiah proclaimed: "And if one look unto the land, behold darkness and sorrow, and the light is darkened in the heavens thereof" (Isaiah 5:30). Jeremiah described the destruction which befell the nation with these words: "I beheld the earth, and, lo, it was without form and void; and the heavens, and they had no light . . . the heavens above be black" (Jeremiah 4:23, 28). Jeremiah warned the Jews to return to God in repentance before "He cause darkness, and before your feet stumble upon the dark mountains, and, while ye look for light he turn it into the shadow of death, and make it gross darkness" (Jeremiah 13:16).

That similar symbolic language was used in reference to Jerusalem's destruction in 70 A.D. can be observed in the words of the prophet Joel:

And it shall come to pass afterward, that I will pour out my spirit upon all flesh; and your sons and your daughters shall prophesy, your old men shall dream dreams, your young men shall see visions: and also upon the servants and upon the handmaids in those days will I pour out my spirit. And I will shew wonders in the heavens and in the earth, blood, and fire, and pillars of smoke. *The sun shall be turned into darkness, and the moon into blood, before the great and the terrible day of the Lord come* (Joel 2:28-31).

Joel not only foretold of the outpouring of the Holy Spirit at Pentecost, but he hinted at the desolation which was coming upon the Jewish nation. In the first part of chapter 2, Joel employs the same familiar, figurative language to describe the judgments coming upon Israel:

The earth shall quake before them; the heavens shall tremble: the sun and the moon shall be dark, and the stars shall withdraw their shining (Joel 2:10).

On the day of Pentecost, Peter informed his listeners that they were witnessing the fulfillment of Joel's prophecy concerning the outpouring of the Holy Ghost (Acts 2:28-32). His sermon implies that the Jews would likewise witness the awesome events symbolically captured in the words of the prophet. These cataclysmic events would transpire with God's judgment being unleashed upon the nation in 70 A.D., resulting in the darkening of Israel's sun, moon, and stars with the collapse of Israel's national existence.

Symbolic Language and the Nations

The same symbolism was employed when describing the turbulence among the Gentile nations as well. In referring to Egypt's destruction by the Babylonian empire we read,

Thus saith the Lord God . . . I will also make the multitude of Egypt to cease by the hand of Nebuchadnezzar . . . he and his people with him . . . shall be brought to destroy the land . . . also the day shall be darkened, when I shall break there the yokes of Egypt . . . as for her, a cloud shall cover her, and her daughters shall go into captivity (Ezekiel 30).

In Ezekiel's prophetic lamentation over Egypt's impending destruction, he wrote:

I will cover the heaven, and make the stars thereof dark; I will cover the sun with a cloud, and the moon shall not give her light. All the bright lights of heaven will I make dark over thee, and set darkness upon the land . . . I shall make the land of Egypt desolate (Ezekiel 32:7-15).

The Babylonian overthrow of Egypt is symbolically portrayed through the figures of the sun, moon, and stars being darkened.

In the same manner, the complete destruction of Idumea (Edom) is symbolically described:

And all the hosts of heaven shall be dissolved, and the heavens shall be rolled together as a scroll; and all their host shall fall down . . . for my sword . . . shall come down upon Idumea . . . to judgment . . . from generation to generation it shall lie waste (Isaiah 34:4-10).

Concerning the destruction of Babylon we read:

He shall destroy the sinners out of it. For the stars of heaven and the constellations thereof shall not give their light: the sun shall be darkened in his going forth, and the moon shall not cause her light to shine . . . I will shake the heavens, and the earth shall remove out of her place, in the wrath of the Lord of hosts, and in the day of his fierce anger. . . . Behold, I will stir up the Medes against them . . . and Babylon . . . shall be as when God overthrew Sodom and Gomorrah . . . it shall never be inhabited, neither shall it be dwelt in from generation to generation (Isaiah 13:9-20).

165

This was literally fulfilled when the Medes and Persians conquered Babylon in 538 B.C. (Daniel 5:25-31). Babylon did in fact become a barren desolation as evidenced by the geographic condition of those lands today.

When Israel was judged, or when Babylon was subdued by the Medes, or when Idumea and Egypt were destroyed, it was not the literal sun, moon, and stars that were darkened. The literal stars of heaven did not fall from the skies, and the literal constellations were not dissolved or rolled up as a scroll. These figurative expressions were clearly presented in a purely symbolic manner to characterize the destruction befalling nations and earthly powers.

The Lord borrowed the language of the prophets to describe the repeated collapse of earthly realms of authority, the upheavals and instability typifying the rise and fall of successive powers, and the continuing series of changes affecting the political sphere. This has been an accurate characterization of the historic plight of this age. Since the cataclysmic events associated with the eclipse of the Jewish nation in 70 A.D., the world has witnessed repeated national, political, and governmental instabilities and turmoil. The "setting of Israel's sun" in 70 A.D. was followed immediately by the ascendancy of a successive series of Gentile powers which have risen and fallen during the extended period we refer to as "the times of the Gentiles."

"The Powers of the Heavens Shall Be Shaken"

Each of the accounts include the statement that "the powers of the heavens shall be shaken." This phrase is intimately linked to the previous mention of signs in the sun, moon, and stars. The words are simply explanatory of what the Lord had spoken concerning the appearance of cosmic disturbances, and demonstrate that He wasn't purposing to convey the thought of literal, physical commotions. In Romans 13:1, we read that "there is no power but from God" when referring to the governmental institutions of earth. Throughout the course of this age, Christ has periodically shaken these powers. In the unfolding process of God's sovereign will being executed in the earth, it has been within God's divine prerogative to shake the nations whenever He pleases.

Christ's words may subtly convey the reality that not only will the church age witness the repetitious cycle of nations in conflict and confusion, but the realm of spiritual powers and principalities will be unsettled and agitated as well. The words "the powers of the heavens shall be shaken" may be a subtle characterization of the ongoing conflict of truth clashing with and undermining the powers of evil in the earth. On a spiritual plane, this phrase depicts the historic confrontation between the kingdom of God and the forces of spiritual deception. The reality of this constant struggle between light and darkness is captured in the words of the Apostle Paul:

> For we wrestle not against flesh and blood, but against principalities, against powers, against the rulers of the darkness of this world, against spiritual wickedness in *high places* (Greek: *epouranios*, heavenly or pertaining to the heavens) (Ephesians 6:12, 13).

These words depict the historic conflict between the church and powers positioned in heavenly realms.

In closing, we might inquire at this point why the Lord would purposely employ such figurative methods of communication when referring to the politcal upheavals characterizing this age. He did so for good reasons. We are strangers and pilgrims in the earth, having no affiliations

167

with the powers that be. However, we are taught to be in subjection to the governments and spheres of authority in the world. His use of figurative language was a discrete way of informing His followers of the truth that the powers of earth were destined to weather a constant state of instability and turmoil. The Lord was cautiously guarding His statements from seeming to convey the idea that His people were somehow intimately connected with the characteristic instability of this age. His symbolism was a prudent way of protecting His people from the potential threat of misunderstanding, and judicial retaliation from the powers which be.

Questions for Discussion

1. Some prophetic speculators point to the alignment of planets such as the "Jupiter effect," or the appearance of comets, eclipses, or meteor storms as signs of the end. How can these phenomena serve as precursory indications of the end when these same phenomena have re-occurred throughout the last two millennia?
2. Can you give any examples of dramatic end-time scenarios which have been fabricated from these verses mentioning signs in the sun, moon, and stars?
3. Accepting the fact that the great tribulation was fulfilled with the judgments of 70 A.D., does the qualifying phrase "*immediately after* the tribulation of those days" contribute to a figurative or literal application of the reference to signs in the heavens?
4. In Luke's parallel account, we are provided information which helps us determine the exact time frame for the phrase "immediately after." Please elaborate.
5. In your opinion, does Luke's statement, "the sea and waves roaring" lend itself more to a figurative or literal

interpretation? Please explain. How is the word *water(s)* used figuratively in the Bible?

6. In Luke 21:25, 26 Jesus characterizes the prevailing sense of fear and malaise plaguing mankind. He employs the word "perplexity," which means "a loss for finding the way." Discuss how humanity has repeatedly reached a place of frustration and impasse in finding the way. Is there a divine purpose built into this perpetual state of bewilderment? Please explain.

7. In Luke 21:26, Christ reveals that men's hearts will fail from fear from observing the distresses of this age. Is there an important lesson in this statement for us? Where should the focus of our attention be—upon the signs of the times, or upon Christ? Please explain. What are some of the detrimental effects of placing our attention upon calamities, whether real or imagined?

8. In your opinion, what does the phrase, "for the powers of heaven shall be shaken" mean?

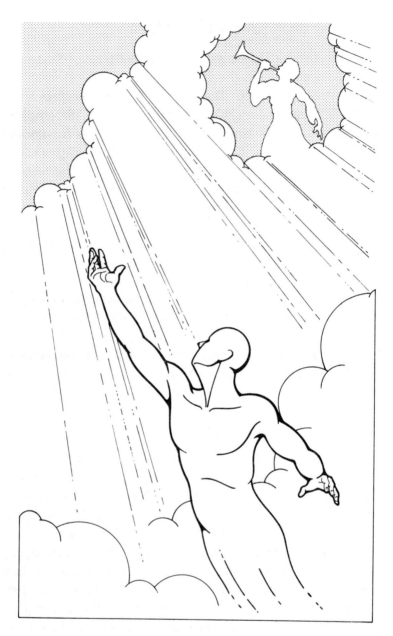

"THE SON OF MAN COMING"

Chapter Eighteen

"THE SON OF MAN COMING"

MATT. 24	MARK 13	LUKE 21
30 And then shall appear the sign of the Son of man in heaven: and then shall all the tribes of the earth mourn, and they shall see the Son of man coming in the clouds of heaven with power and great glory.	26 And then shall they see the Son of man coming in the clouds with great power and glory.	27 And then shall they see the Son of man coming in a cloud with power and great glory.
31 And he shall send his angels with a great sound of a trumpet, and they shall gather together his elect from the four winds, from one end of heaven to the other.	27 And then shall he send his angels, and shall gather together his elect from the four winds, from the uttermost part of the earth to the uttermost part of heaven.	

The thought of Christ suddenly bursting through the clouds with power and glory, accompanied by the angelic host, and heralded by the sound of a mighty trumpet is one which stirs the hearts of each of us. The second coming will be the greatest prophetic event in all history. It is one which the church has longed for and eagerly anticipated for centuries.

A Figurative Coming?

In the course of Christ's panoramic survey of this age, He now touches upon this glorious theme. After figuratively alluding to the general instability which was to characterize this age, Jesus now comes to the final event on the prophetic calendar—His visible return in power and majesty.

However, not all expositors are in agreement in applying these passages to a second coming scenario. Some scholars interpret these statements in a strictly figurative manner and see in them an obvious reference to the coming of Christ in power and judgment upon the nation of Israel in 70 A.D. For example, George Murray stated:

171

It is not surprising that this clause ["they shall see the Son of man coming in the clouds of heaven with power and great glory,"] is so generally accepted as referring to the Lord's return, for that seems to be the obvious meaning . . . We take second place to no one in our conviction that the Lord will return personally and visibly, but we cannot blind ourselves to the fact that on this occasion He was using Old Testament figures of speech.[1]

In defending this position, some cite the similar wording in Christ's warnings to the Sanhedrin on the eve of His crucifixion:

Jesus saith unto him, Thou hast said: nevertheless I say unto you, Hereafter shall ye see the Son of man sitting on the right hand of power, and coming in the clouds of heaven (Matthew 26:64).

Those who lean towards this persuasion see in these statements a symbolic reference to His coming in judgment against the Jewish nation.

Advocates of this perspective are quick to point out Old Testament symbolism which speaks of the Lord's coming. In Genesis 11:5 we read: "The Lord *came down* to see the city." The scriptures speak of the Lord *coming* to men in their dreams (Genesis 20:3). In Exodus 3:8 we read, "I am *come down* to deliver them." The psalmist wrote, "He shall *come down* like rain upon the mown grass" (Psalm 72:6). David spoke of the Lord's assistance in battle saying, "The Lord . . . bowed the heavens . . . and *came down* . . . he delivered me" (Psalm 18:6-17). The prophet Isaiah stated, "So shall the Lord of hosts *come down* to fight for Mount Zion, and for the hill thereof" (Isaiah 31:4). In the context of Israel's restoration to their homeland after their Babylonian

---

1. George Murray, *Millennial Studies*, p. 123.

captivity, God said, "I am *returned* unto Jerusalem" (Zechariah 1:16; 8:3). These represent a few selected verses characterizing the Lord's coming in a purely symbolic fashion. Most would readily agree that these verses are not literal references to a personal, visible return of the Lord at the end of this age.

With these scriptural precedents, some expositors believe that we should interpret these Olivet passages in the same figurative context. They interpret the mention of the sending forth of angels and the sounding of the trumpets in the sense of God's sending forth His messengers to sound forth the clarion call of the gospel message in order to gather His elect from the uttermost parts of the earth. They interpret the phrase "coming in the clouds" symbolically as well. For example, Matthew Henry stated,

> The destruction of Jerusalem was in a particular manner an act of Christ's judgment, the judgment committed to the Son of man . . . it might justly be looked upon as a coming of the Son of man, in power and great glory, yet not visibly in the clouds.[2]

They also appeal to the scriptures for support. In Exodus 19:9 we read: "Lo, I come unto thee in a thick cloud." In Exodus 34:5 we read: "The Lord descended in the cloud, and stood with him there." Other scriptures speak of the Lord "riding upon a swift cloud" (Isaiah 19:1; see also Psalms 18:10 and 104:3). Psalms 97:2 speaks of "clouds and darkness (being) round about him."

In spite of these appeals to similar Old Testament phraseology, I still find this interpretive position encountering insurmountable obstacles at this particular point in the prophecy. Though I strongly contend that the major emphasis

---

2. Matthew Henry, *Matthew Henry's Commentary*, Vol. 5.

of the Olivet discourse has thus far focused primarily upon the events directly associated with Israel's destruction in 70 A.D. and not to the secondary subject of the end of the age, I do disagree with those who forcefully attempt to apply a figurative interpretation upon the clear thrust of these verses. It is my studied opinion that these expositors have pushed the historic perspective a bit too far in attempting to force the intended meaning of these passages into the straitjacket of 70 A.D.

Jesus had, indeed, figuratively characterized the distinctive features of this age (political unrest, international instability, etc.) in the preceding verses (Matthew 24:29; Mark 13:24, 25; Luke 21:25, 26). But, in the sequential order of events, He had clearly stated that these things would commence *immediately after* the tribulation of those days (Matthew 24:29) and, by implication, these symbolic highlights of the course of this age would extend to the very end when Christ would literally return in power and great glory. The passages under consideration simply present the great prophetic capstone of this age—the Second Coming of Christ. The language is clear and straightforward regarding this fact. I find serious limitations and contextual weaknesses when endeavoring to force a symbolic interpretation upon the distinctive wording of these verses.

When compared with similar passages in the epistles which are clearly related to the second coming, I find that the earnest attempts to limit the application of these particular verses to the confines of the events surrounding Jerusalem's destruction falling somewhat short.

"Coming in the Clouds"

In these Olivet passages we read, "They shall *see* the Son of man *coming in the clouds* of heaven with power and great glory" (Matthew 24:30). This wording corresponds with the noted second coming passage of Revelation 1:7:

> Behold, he *cometh with the clouds;* and every eye shall *see* him . . . and all kindred of the earth shall wail because of him.

In both passages, we are told that the Lord will be seen and that His coming will be associated with clouds. When Christ ascended to the Father, we are told that "a CLOUD received him out of their sight" (Acts 1:9), and that when He returns again He "shall so come in like manner (in the clouds) as ye have seen him go into heaven" (Acts 1:11). In I Thessalonians 4:17 we are informed that when Jesus returns, believers will be "caught up . . . in the CLOUDS, to meet the Lord in the air."

Angels and a Trumpet

These Olivet passages also state that He shall send His angels forth to gather the elect with a sound of a great trumpet. In two of the most familiar second coming passages, the sounding of the trumpet is closely connected with the Lord's return (see I Thessalonians 4:16; I Corinthians 15:52). Angels are repeatedly mentioned in the context of the second coming. For example, in II Thessalonians 1:7 we read:

> And to you who are troubled rest with us, when the Lord Jesus shall be revealed from heaven with his mighty ANGELS (see also Matthew 16:27; Matthew 25:31; Luke 9:26).

In Matthew 13:24-30 and 36-43 we read that at the end of the world the angels of God will be dispatched to reap the harvest. They will be commissioned to gather the wicked for destruction and the righteous for everlasting life.

175

The Gathering of the Elect

In Matthew and Mark's Olivet accounts, we are told that the elect shall be gathered together "from the four winds, from one end of heaven to the other." This statement cannot possibly be limited to the geographic area of Palestine alone. There is an inherent universality inferred through the wording which agrees with the scriptural characterization of the Lord's return when *all* the tribes of the earth shall see Him, and not just the inhabitants of Judea. It should be further noted that "all the tribes of the earth" did not mourn because of the divinely orchestrated judgments upon Israel in 66-70 A.D. The awesome tribulation of those days was limited to the Palestinian Jews:

> For there shall be great distress *in the land* (Palestine, and not the entire world) and wrath upon *this people* (the rebellious nation of Jewry) (Luke 21:23b).

In a limited sense, God did indeed come in judgment upon the Jewish nation in 70 A.D., but to restrict the application of these particular Olivet statements to the narrow confines of that tragic event would be a breach of sound exegesis, especially when viewed against the New Testament backdrop of similar passages which are clearly set in a second coming context.

With these insights in mind, I support the interpretive position which applies Matthew 24:30, 31 (and the parallel verses) to a second coming context, and not to a figurative coming in judgment in 70 A.D. These parallel passages are in perfect accord with other New Testament descriptions of the second coming, when He shall come in the clouds with power and great glory; when men shall behold Him and mourn; and when He shall send forth the angelic host with the voice of the archangel and the trumpet of God to gather the believers from the ends of the earth.

"The Sign of the Son of Man"

I should note that the wording of these passages includes the phrase: "And then shall appear the *sign* of the Son of man in heaven" (Matthew 24:30). This statement does not imply that there will be some extraordinary cosmic sign to prepare the world for the Lord's advent. As I have repeatedly stressed, the scriptures are emphatic in the assertion that there will be no obvious, preliminary signs to announce to an unsuspecting world that the second coming is imminent. This phrase simply suggests that at the actual timing of the second coming, the sign of the Son of man (Jesus) will appear in the heavens. All that this expression is inferring is that Jesus Christ will be clearly manifested in the heavens in conjunction with His descent to earth in glory. This passage is not referring to some subtle or mysterious revelation of the Son of man prior to his open revelation. The word *appear* (Greek: *phaino*) signifies "to be brought forth into light, to become evident, to appear." As I have stated, though His coming will be unannounced and instantaneous, it will be as bold and patent as a flash of lightning. In harmony with the context of the entire thrust of the Olivet prophecy, the implication of this phrase is that there will be no unmistakable, visible signs to herald the timing of His impending coming, and that the only sign given will be the manifestation of His person at the actual moment of His coming in glory.

"Then"

In closing, I should consider a serious objection to the chronological order which I have presented concerning this

177

division of the Olivet prophecy. As we observed in the previous section, the scriptures depicted the cosmic events which were to transpire "immediately after the tribulation of those days" (Matthew 24:29). The discourse follows immediately with the statement that, "And THEN shall appear the sign of the Son of man in heaven . . . and they shall see the Son of man coming in the clouds of heaven, with power and great glory" (Matthew 24:30). At first glance, the word *then* would seem to strongly suggest that the second coming was to follow *immediately after* the tribulation of those days. Because of this, and in spite of the strong scriptural and historical proofs to the contrary, many expositors apply the tribulation to a strict end-time setting. They hold that the "Great Tribulation" will be consummated with the second coming of Christ. This assumption is based strongly upon the context of the word *then.* This word is derived from the Greek word *tote.* Matthew uses this word more than all the other New Testament authors put together (90 times). It is flexible in that it can either indicate something which is to happen at a specific time, or it can be used in a far more general sense to indicate the sequence in which a series of events will happen. That order could either happen immediately, or be separated by a great span of time. I believe that Jesus was employing the word *tote* to explain the order in which events would occur rather than attempting to place the second coming immediately after the tribulation which He refers to in the Olivet discourse. The order of events which is presented in verses 29-31 is: 1) tribulation upon the nation of Israel, 2) followed *immediately* by an extended period characterized by unrest and instability among the nations, and 3) *then* ending with the second coming of Christ in power and glory.

Questions for Discussion

1. Does the descriptive wording of Matthew 24:31 lend itself to the dispensationalist's teaching of a secret pre-tribulation rapture? Why?
2. In your opinion, when will Matthew 26:64 be fulfilled?
3. List as many Bible passages as you can referring to a literal, physical second coming of Christ.
4. Can you provide any other interpretations of the phrase "the sign of the Son of man in heaven"?

"LIFT UP YOUR HEADS"

Chapter Nineteen

"LIFT UP YOUR HEADS!"

MATT. 24	MARK 13	LUKE 21
		28 And when these things begin to come to pass, then look up, and lift up your heads; for your redemption draweth nigh.

How was the church to react to the turbulence of this age? Was it to be one of anxiety and despair, or hopeful expectation? Against the backdrop of the chaotic conditions affecting the entire gauntlet of this age, the Lord provided a timeless encouragement for His people to undergird them in their hour of need.

This isolated encouragement is only found in Luke's account. Christ stresses that when His followers first observed *these things* beginning to transpire, they were to recognize that their inevitable deliverance was drawing near. Several views have been offered in an attempt to establish the precise application of this statement. Two significant phrases call for careful consideration: they are "these things," and "begin to come to pass." In order to establish an accurate interpretation of this verse, we must first determine what exactly *these things* refer to, and when did these things *begin*?

The Timing of These Things

The predominant view holds that this passage is inseparably connected with the preceding information involving the second coming (Luke 21:27). This school maintains that *these things* are intimately linked to the catastrophic upheavals and cosmic portents which will supposedly accompany the final events at the close of the age. Many view the supposed emergence of celestial phenomena and the outbreak of worldwide disturbances in the context of God's final outpouring of wrath during a distinct period of worldwide trauma known as the "Great Tribulation." They interpret this passage as Christ's revelation that the last generation of believers will be able to clearly determine the approximate timing of the end by means of the distinctive signs manifested in the heavens and the unparalleled worldwide calamities upon earth. For example, Geldenhuys states:

> Before the end of the age, all creation and the whole of the human world will be plunged into dreadful commotions—in the sun, the moon, and the stars there will appear miraculous and alarming signs, the whole life of the nations on earth will be disrupted through the anxiety and terror that will overwhelm the people and render them desperate.[1]

Those that hold this position view these words of encouragement in a strict end-time context. They maintain that Christ's challenging exhortation was directed solely towards that final generation of believers living in the midst of a chaotic world seized in a state of unprecendented terror and confusion.

However, I feel that this is an untenable position which is clearly negated by Christ's additional comments. When viewed in the contextual light of the entire prophecy, the assumption that this verse (Luke 21:28) must apply strictly to a last days time frame falls flat. It is highly improbable that the mention of "these things" refers directly to the emergence of precursory, cataclysmic events towards the consummation of this age, for, this is in diametric opposition to Christ's lucid revelations to the contrary.

---

1. Norval Geldenhuys, *Commentary on Luke*, p. 538.

The prevalent notion that the prophetic calendar of events must witness the dramatic outbreak of preliminary signs to clearly herald the return of Christ runs cross-grain to the straightforward statements of Jesus. He emphatically informed His disciples that *no man* would *know* the timing of His advent (Matthew 24:36). In fact, in Mark's Olivet version, He forcefully stressed:

Take heed, watch and pray: *for ye know not when the time is* (Mark 13:33).

Though I'm not presumptuously denying the possibility that there will be varying degrees of turbulence towards the end, I do hold that the frequency of such occurrences throughout the entire course of this age forbids any calamities from serving as obvious indicators of the nearness of His return. If Jesus pointedly stated that NO man would know ("know," Greek: *eido* - to know, be sure of, aware of, perceive, see, understand, tell, or to know from observation), then NO man will be able to clearly distinguish, perceive, be sure of, aware of, or be able to know for certain when the climax of this age will transpire.

The Lord's statements on this point are most emphatic. The end will be shrouded in uncertainty until the very moment when it strikes like a "thief in the night" (Matthew 24:42-44). The internal statements contained within the whole of this prophecy concerning this crucial prophetic point absolutely govern our interpretation concerning the supposed manifestation of obvious endtime portents. With this perspective in mind, I maintain that the timing when *these things* will begin to occur has no exclusive bearing upon the final events of this age.

183

A Timeless Encouragement

However, if *these things* refer to the general instability and distresses which were predicted to characterize the entire course of this age, then, as we have previously emphasized, their initial emergence commenced shortly after Christ's Mount Olivet discourse, and have continued to this day. In this case, the time when these things began to come to pass commenced at the begining of this age. In this context, these words of encouragement are intended to provide believers of every generation with a positive air of assurance in spite of the duresses they would endure. The exhortation to "look up, and lift up your heads" has a broad application for all Christians of every generation, stirring and admonishing them to maintain a hopeful and expectant outlook regardless of the peculiar distresses affecting their particular moment in history.

In contrast to the worldwide state of consternation and fear gripping the hearts of unregenerate humanity, Christians are exhorted to remain confident and unwavering in the face of turmoil. Against the backdrop of the increasing presence of wars and rumors of wars, Jesus had previously stressed to His followers, "Be not afraid" (Luke 21:9). At no point in history should Christians falter from fear or confusion due to the calamities surrounding them. The church must never succumb to an anxious foreboding of future events—real or imagined. Christians have always been challenged to raise their sights and observe the calamities and tribulations of this age against the positive backdrop of our ultimate deliverance. We must never be overwhelmed by fearfully dwelling upon "those things which are coming on the earth" (Luke 21:26). In spite of the distinctive distresses which each age has produced, Christians must repeatedly guard themselves from being more "event-centered" than "Christ-centered" in their world view.

Each generation has been instructed to remain hopeful and vigilant in spite of the uncertainty surrounding the timing of Christ's return. These specific words of encouragement have bolstered the faith of Christians throughout the breadth of this age with the positive expectation of their eventual deliverance. This encouragement equally applies to those believers living in the final stage of this dispensation, as well as to the innumerable company of saints who have already come and gone. We will all share in the blessed hope of the second coming of Christ.

In the final analysis, in spite of the fact that the exact timing of Christ's return has always been shrouded in uncertainty, each generation of believers has been sustained by Luke's promise and encouraged to stand fast in this crucial attitude of hopeful expectancy, "in this present world, looking for that blessed hope, and the glorious appearing of the great God and our Saviour Jesus Christ" (Titus 2:12, 13). This has been the constant watchword of the church. As Alan Cole so aptly commented:

> In seeing the Lord's return as always just around the corner, the infant church was doing no wrong. So they should have done and so should we; for every generation should be eagerly looking for and expecting the Lord's coming.[2]

The church has always lived in the consciousness that "the end of all things is at hand" (Phil. 4:5; James 5:9; I Pet. 4:7a).

A Partial Fulfillment

In closing, I should point out that Luke's isolated statement is closely linked to the detailed information which the

---

2. Alan Cole, *Gospel According to Mark*, p. 206.

Lord had so painstakenly entrusted to *that* generation of Jewish believers concerning Jerusalem's impending desolation and the distinct signs which were to precede that event. In all probability, the disciples were being exhorted that when they observed *these things* beginning to transpire, they were to lift up their heads in the confident awareness that their redemption drew near. When the Christian community of Palestine witnessed the manifest appearance of the approaching "abomination of desolation," they could take courage in the awareness that their tangible deliverance was near.

The Lord had carefully provided them with the necessary instructions in order to facilitate their safe exodus before the actual holocaust. In the case of the Christians inhabiting Judea and Jerusalem during the distresses of 66-70 A.D., this promise was literally fulfilled. What is more, the Lord had revealed to them that those days would indeed be shortened for the sake of the *elect.* This was Christ's positive word of assurance that they would be spared from the terrors that were soon destined to engulf the Jewish nation. They were comforted in the awareness that they would not perish in the Roman war of extermination. In this context, Luke's statement finds at least a partial, literal fulfillment.

Questions for Discussion

1. List other New Testament passages which also exhort the church to find faith and hope in the midst of tribulations.
2. Are we justified in confining this exhortation to the last day church?

186

3. Does this verse have a practical application in our lives even when we face personal times of tribulation and distress? Please explain.
4. Discuss what the deeper implications of the expression "lift up your heads" are.
5. Do you feel that this passage was partially fulfilled in 70 A.D.? Please explain. Can you provide an example where it has been fulfilled since?

"BEHOLD THE FIG TREE!"

Chapter Twenty

"BEHOLD THE FIG TREE!"

MATT. 24	MARK 13	LUKE 21
32 Now learn a parable of the fig tree; When his branch is yet tender, and putteth forth leaves, ye know that summer is nigh:	28 Now learn a parable of the fig tree; When her branch is yet tender, and putteth forth leaves, ye know that summer is near:	29 And he spake to them a parable; Behold the fig tree, and all the trees;
33 So likewise ye, when ye shall see all these things, know that it is near, *even* at the doors.	29 So ye in like manner, when ye shall see these things come to pass, know that it is nigh, *even* at the doors.	30 When they now shoot forth, ye see and know of your own selves that summer is now nigh at hand.
34 Verily I say unto you, This generation shall not pass, till all these things be fulfilled.	30 Verily I say unto you, that this generation shall not pass, till all these things be done.	31 So likewise ye, when ye see these things come to pass, know ye that the kingdom of God is nigh at hand.
35 Heaven and earth shall pass away, but my words shall not pass away.	31 Heaven and earth shall pass away: but my words shall not pass away.	32 Verily I say unto you, This generation shall not pass away, till all be fulfilled.
		33 Heaven and earth shall pass away: but my words shall not pass away.

Many view the fig tree parable as a veiled, symbolic reference to the physical nation of Israel. Many contend that Christ employed this parable to foreshadow prophetically the rebirth of the Jewish nation, as well as provide a failsafe means of approximating the timing of His return. But was this the intended meaning of this simple parable?

Israel and the Fig Tree

We often hear that the "budding of the fig tree" has a direct prophetic link to the re-establishment of Jewish statehood in 1948. This school claims that since Christ clearly stated that *that* generation (the one living when Israel regains her statehood) would not pass away until all be fulfilled (Matthew 24:34), that the fig tree parable guarantees that our generation will not expire until it witnesses the Second Coming. Since a generation, in biblical terms, spans approximately forty years, some have boldly gone so far as to predict the Lord's coming no later than 1988!

189

But in spite of the widespread popularity attending this opinion, there is absolutely no guarantee in this parable, or anywhere else in the scriptures, proving that our present generation will or will not witness the Second Coming of Christ. Furthermore, I must question whether Christ intended in any way, shape or form to apply the thrust of this parable to the end of the age, or tie it to the restoration of the Jewish nation.

There is little biblical support for the contention that the fig tree is a clear-cut and consistently employed symbol for the physical nation of Israel. However, advocates of this interpretive position frequently appeal to two New Testament passages in particular as supposed "proof texts" of the fact that the fig tree indeed symbolizes natural Israel.

In the parable of the "vinedresser and the fig tree" we read:

> He spake also this parable: A certain man had a fig tree planted in his vineyard, and he came and sought fruit thereon, and found none. Then said he unto the dresser of his vineyard, Behold, these three years I come seeking fruit on this fig tree, and find none: cut it down; why cumbereth it the ground? And he answering said unto him, Lord, let it alone this year also, till I shall dig about it, and dung it: and if it bear fruit, well; and if not, then after that thou shalt cut it down (Luke 13:6-9).

There is nothing implied in this parable to indicate that the fig tree ever became fruitful. If we accept this parable as a subtle reference to the Jewish nation which Christ personally ministered to for over three years, we know that the Israelite nation, as a whole, did not bear the fruits of repentance (Matthew 3:8). But contrawise, they spurned the extended mercies of God and, according to the prophetic declarations of Christ, were cut off and destroyed in 70 A.D.

190

Another fig tree passage referred to in reference to Israel is Matthew 21:19:

> And when he saw a fig tree in the way, he came to it, and found nothing thereon, but leaves only, and said unto it, Let no fruit grow on these henceforward for ever. And presently the fig tree withered away.

It should be noted that the fig tree in question was cursed by Christ when He proclaimed, "Let no fruit grow on thee henceforward for ever!" If anything is to be inferred from the thrust of this incident, it is that the fig tree would never bud again. So, if we hold that the fig tree reference in this verse has a direct application to the national status of Israel, then we must accept Christ's additional revelation that the fig tree will never blossom "henceforth for ever." Both of these passages fall short from adequately providing the expositor with substantial support that the fig tree is an obvious, symbolic representation of the physical state of Israel.

The only indicative passages in the New Testament which symbolically liken Israel unto a tree are located in Romans 11:17, 24; however, Israel is not compared to a fig tree in these verses, but to an olive tree! In examining these scriptures, we can readily see that the Bible does not dogmatically enforce the symbolism of the fig tree upon the national capacity of Israel.

"All the Trees"

Though each of the Olivet prophecies include the fig tree text, only Luke's version includes the words:

> Behold the fig tree AND ALL THE TREES (Luke 21:29).

191

Luke broadens the general scope of this parable to include "all the trees." In spite of this fact, some dispensationalists still insist upon circumventing this detail by claiming that though the fig tree refers to Israel's restored statehood in 1948, the expression "all the trees" is a prophetic characterization of the worldwide de-colonialization of numerous nations during the post World War II era of the 40's and 50's. They link the budding of "all the trees" to the emergence of the many independent nations of Asia and Africa in the aftermath of World War II. They see this international phenomenon coinciding with the regained national identity of Israel. Though these arguments may serve as convenient supports for applying the fig tree to the restored statehood of Israel, I must ask if this was actually the intended thrust of Christ's fig tree parable.

Many learned expositors dismiss this theory as little more than groundless speculation. Even Dake, who was an avid dispensationalist, stated:

> The fig tree . . . is universally interpreted to mean the Jewish nation, but this could not possibly be the meaning . . . to use a few leaves to represent certain events of Israel is just as unscriptural as to pick a few oak leaves to represent truths about Gentiles.[1]

Likewise, Geldenhuys forcefully asserted that:

> It is quite impermissible to take the fig tree here as a symbol of the Jewish people and to teach that a revival of the Jewish national life of Palestine is meant. For the words used here are not merely "Behold the fig tree," but also "and all the trees."[2]

Ellison also commented: "It is not permissible to equate the fig tree with the Jews; it is never so used elsewhere."[3]

---

1. Finis J. Dake, *Dake's Annotated Reference Bible*, p. 27.
2. Norval Geldenhuys, *The Gospel of Luke*, p. 541.
3. H. L. Ellison, *The New Laymen's Bible Commentary*, p. 1213.

What Things?

Jesus was simply drawing a lesson from nature. When they first observed the fig tree and all the trees of the field beginning to bud, they knew by common knowledge that the advent of summer was near:

> So ye in like manner, when ye shall see *these things* come to pass, know that it is nigh, even at the doors (Mark 13:29).

Jesus was appealing to basic human logic. When trees put forth their leaves, men comprehend that the summer season is rapidly approaching. Likewise, when the disciples of that generation witnessed all *these things* coming to pass, then they would know that the event which Jesus had so carefully instructed them about would soon take place.

Many apply the reference of *these things* to a strict end-time setting. They hold that *these things* refer to the cosmic portents and unprecedented catastrophies which will sweep the earth as preparatory signals of the world's end. But is this parable a continuation of what Jesus had just spoken of concerning His second coming (Matthew 24:30, 31), or was He in fact returning to His original line of thought concerning the predicted events which were to alert *that* generation of the impending desolation of Jerusalem? Do *these things* involve the supposed spectacular events at the end of the age, or are they referring to the events preceding Israel's destruction in 70 A.D.?

In regards to this point, Edersheim noted:

> From the fig tree, under which, on that spring afternoon they may have rested on the Mount of Olives, they were to learn a "parable." We can picture Christ taking one of its twigs, just as its softening tips were bursting into young leaf. Surely, this meant that summer was nigh—not that it had

actually come. The distinction is important. For it seems to prove that "all these things," which were to indicate to them that it was near, even at the doors, and which were to be fulfilled ere this generation had passed away, could not have referred to the last signs connected with the immediate Advent of Christ, but must apply to the previous prediction of the destruction of Jerusalem, and of the Jewish commonwealth.[4]

If we adopt a futurist position which applies "all these things" to everything that Jesus had just previously mentioned, the passage would then imply this:

> When you see the sun darkened, the moon not giving light, the stars falling, the powers of heaven shaken, the sign of the Son of man in heaven, all the tribes of earth mourning, the Son of man coming in the clouds, the sound of the trumpet, the final gathering of the elect: when you shall see *all* these things, then recognize that the very end is near.

However, this rendering is insensible, for it suggests that when the disciples saw the Lord coming in the clouds, then they would know that the second coming was near. As J. Marcellus Kik so appropriately stated:

> Imagine Christ telling His disciples that when they saw Him coming in the clouds then they would know that His second coming was at the doors! Imagine Christ telling His disciples that when they saw Him sending His angels with a great sound of the trumpet to gather the elect from the four winds then they would know His second coming was at the doors.[5]

This rendering is simply contrary to basic logic and commonsense.

I therefore maintain that the phrase "these things" refers to the distinctive events which that generation of Jewish

---

4. Alfred Edersheim, *The Life and Times of Jesus the Messiah*, p. 450.
5. Marcellus Kik, *Matthew Twenty-Four — An Exposition*, p. 83.

Christians would observe in close conjunction with the destruction of Jerusalem. Jesus had carefully warned them of the more general disturbances (i.e., wars, rumors of wars, famines, pestilences, earthquakes, persecution). He had concluded by revealing the specific sign of Jerusalem being surrounded by foreign armies (Luke 21:20, 21). When they observed "these things," especially the unmistakable sign of the "abomination that maketh desolate," they could safely conclude that Jerusalem's destruction was near.

> Jesus is here saying in effect that it will be as certain that Jerusalem will fall when all these things (i.e., the appearance of the abomination of desolation, the advent of false Messiahs, etc.) have become apparent, as it is certain that summer will follow when the first leaves are seen on the fig tree's tender branches.[6]

The budding of the fig tree was a harbinger of summer as these signs were to be of Jerusalem's impending desolation.

It is interesting to note that in the natural course of seasons, several months actually separate the bursting forth of the first buds of the fig tree in early spring, and the fulness of summer in August. So too, the abomination of desolation appeared in early spring of 70 A.D., the siege of Jerusalem was engaged in April, and the temple was burnt in fulfillment of Christ's prophecy on August 10th, 70 A.D.

A Generation

Christ further stated that:

> . . . this GENERATION shall not pass till all these things be fulfilled.

The precise determination of the intended timing of this parable rests fundamentally upon the meaning of the word

---

6. R.V.G. Tasker, *The Gospel According to St. Matthew*, p. 227.

generation. The exact application of the word *generation* is absolutely crucial to an accurate exegesis of this division of the prophecy. If Christ's clear-cut declaration that "this generation shall not pass away until all these things be ful-filled" was in direct reference to *that* generation of disciples which He was personally addressing, then an end-time appli-cation of this parable and "these things" is completely undermined.

Recognizing this glaring point, many expositors have sought to evade the obvious thrust of this verse (Matthew 24:34) by substituting another meaning for the word *generation.* In attempting to force this section of the discourse into a second coming context, some expositors have adopted the "doubtful expedient" of stretching the word *generation* to mean a race of people in their successive capacity. Others have interpreted the word generation to mean "a people." Some substitute the word "nation" or "Israel" or "stock" or "family." But the scriptures provide no warrant for sup-porting the notion that the word *generation* was used to convey the idea of a nation in its successive generations. As Plummer stated,

> Here, as elsewhere in the gospels, this expression can hardly mean anything else than Christ's own contemporaries. To make it mean the Jewish race, or the race of believers, or the whole race of mankind, is not satisfactory. [7]

This "open-ended" use of the word is totally unwarranted and unscriptural. This interpretation has only been adopted in order to force the "fig tree" division of the prophecy into a futuristic framework of prophetic interpretation.

This point of view does not measure up when we examine the other scriptural uses of the word *generation* found in Matthew's gospel. For example, in Matthew 1:17 we read:

---

7. Alfred Plummer, *The Gospel According to St. Mark,* p. 305.

> So all the generations from Abraham to David are fourteen *generations*; and from David until the carrying away into Babylon are fourteen *generations*; and from the carrying away into Babylon unto Christ are fourteen *generations*.

The obvious reference of this passage is to 42 distinct generations which followed each other in logical, chronological sequence, and not to one endless generation stretching for hundreds of years. Neither does the word subtly convey the meaning of 42 "races" or "nations."

In Matthew 11:16 we read:

> But whereunto shall I liken this *generation*? It is like unto children sitting in the markets, and calling unto their fellows.

In the context of this statement, Jesus was rebuking that very generation of Jews for rejecting the ministry of John the Baptist and for deriding Jesus. It was not Israel in her successive capacity of generations who were mocking John and leveling their criticisms against Christ, but that present generation.

The word *generation* is employed four times in Matthew 12:38-45. Jesus was strongly rebuking the Jews in these passages. He labeled them "an evil and adulterous generation" which was seeking for a sign. He revealed to them that the only sign which would be given them would be the sign of Jonah the prophet (see also Matthew 16:4). This sign was none other than the death, burial, and resurrection of Christ which would occur in their generation. It should be stressed that only that single generation actually witnessed this sign.

He further added that "The men of Ninevah shall rise in judgment with this generation, and shall condemn it" (verse 41). He stated that *that* generation of Jews would be condemned because they repented not at the preaching of one

197

greater than Jonah (Jesus). In the same text, Jesus likened that generation to a demon-possessed man whose "last state was worse than the first" (verse 45), and added that "even so shall it be unto this wicked generation." This is in keeping with Christ's final denunciation against the ecclesiastical authorities when He declared that they had filled up the measure of their fathers (Matthew 23:32). It was that generation who had brought the cup of God's wrath to the brim. It was that generation of Jews which was accurately characterized as being worse than all the preceding generations, for it was that generation which was actually responsible for crucifying the Son of God.

In His last indictment against the nation, He declared:

> Ye serpents, ye generation of vipers, how can ye escape the damnation of hell? . . . Verily I say unto you, All these things shall come upon THIS GENERATION (Matthew 23:33, 36).

That that very generation of Jews did experience the wrath of God is an undeniable historic fact, and this sobering revelation harmonizes perfectly with Matthew 24:34 in which Jesus re-emphasizes the truth: "Verily I say unto you, THIS GENERATION shall not pass till all these things be fulfilled!"

"All These Things"

He had instructed His disciples by means of the fig tree parable that when they saw "all these things" they were to recognize that the predicted desolation of the city was very near. The mention of "these things" is a direct reference to the unmistakable signs which He had so carefully provided them as early warnings to facilitate their safe exodus (i.e., rise of false Christs and abomination of desolation). He then added the guarantee that:

> Verily I say unto you, THIS GENERATION shall not pass till ALL THESE THINGS be fulfilled (Matthew 24:34).

It should be noted that the fig tree text employs the phrase "all these things" twice (Matthew 24:33, 34). The first reference is to the signs which were to immediately precede Jerusalem's destruction, and the second is in reference to the actual destruction which would befall the nation.

In the midst of His severe denunciations against the Jewish leaders, He had stated that "all these things" would overtake that generation (Matthew 23:31-38). The judgment which was coming would include the desolation of the temple (Matthew 23:38). When exiting the temple, Jesus repeated the phrase "all these things" in conjunction with His startling revelation concerning the temple's destruction (Matthew 24:2). It is obvious that the phrase "all these things" refers to the tragic events accompanying Jerusalem's destruction. When the disciples approached Jesus for a fuller explanation of His startling statements involving the temple's destruction, they inquired:

> . . . Tell us, when shall THESE THINGS be? And what shall be the sign of thy coming, and of the end of the world?

Christ had just employed this expression in conjunction with the temple's destruction (Matthew 24:2), and in His pronouncements of woe upon the religious authorities (Matthew 23:36, 38); so, naturally, the disciples had in mind those same awesome events when they asked Jesus when "all these things" were slated to transpire.

Christ employed the parable of the fig tree in direct response to their inquiries. In it, He first stated that when the disciples witnessed "all these things" (the preceding signs), they were to know without a doubt that the destruction was about to befall the city: ". . . know that it is near, even at the doors" (Matthew 24:33). He then added the guarantee that "all these things," that is, the actual desolation of Jerusalem would happen before that present generation expired. As He had previously used the phrase "all these things" in reference to the declaration of woes against the scribes and Pharisees, and in reference to the temple's actual destruction (Matthew 23), He does so also in this section of the fig tree text.

The disciples had pointedly asked Him when "all these things" would be fulfilled, and in response to their question, the Lord bluntly affirmed that "all these things" would happen within their generation (Matthew 24:34). To assume anything else than this simple application of the fig tree parable only confuses the intended thrust of Christ's reply.

The proof that Christ's predictions were literally fulfilled in that generation can be seen in the fact that the awesome judgments which befell Israel actually transpired within forty years of Christ's statements. From the timing of Christ's last words to the nation in approximately 30 A.D., God afforded the Jewish nation a forty year probationary period which expired with the judgments of 70 A.D. So, in perfect harmony with Jesus' predictions, that generation lived to witness "all these things" before passing from the scene of history. As if to forcefully seal the certainty of His predictions concerning the fate of *that* generation of Jews, He added the divine assurance that:

Heaven and earth shall pass away, but my words shall not pass away (Matthew 24:35; see also Mark 13:31 and Luke 21:33).

200

All that He had prophesied concerning the wrath which would fall upon that generation was irrevocable and absolute.

"The Kingdom of God is Nigh at Hand"

Before concluding this section of the prophecy, I should give brief attention to a phrase found only in Luke's account:

So likewise ye, when ye see these things come to pass, know ye that THE KINGDOM OF GOD IS NIGH AT HAND (Luke 21:31).

On the surface, the phrase "the kingdom of God is nigh at hand" seems to contradict the position I have just taken. Many view this statement as an obvious reference to the manifestation of Christ's kingdom at His second coming. However, in view of the parallel context in which it is found, as well as the strong supports which overwhelmingly demonstrate that the fig tree parable is directly related to the events of 70 A.D., I see another meaning implied through this statement.

Jesus noted that *that* generation would endure until the terrors of 70 A.D. overtook them. That forty year probationary period was a time of unique transition in the early stage of the church's history. It was a period which experienced the overlapping of two dispensations. They were years of great difficulty for the fledgling church. During this period, the church repeatedly weathered the persistent opposition of Judaistic pressures from the outside, as well as from within the church ranks itself. The gospel of grace was repeatedly challenged by the vigorous and determined assaults of the Jews. This confrontation is repeatedly mentioned in the scriptures (Acts 15, Galatians, II Corinthians, etc.). But with Jerusalem's destruction in 70 A.D., the last bastion of

Judaism was eliminated and the break with the old dispensation was final and complete.

> Henceforth the nascent Gentile church was not hampered by intolerant and exclusive Judaistic tendencies fostered in Jerusalem. . . . The destruction of Jerusalem assisted in breaking down the partition between "Jew" and "Gentile" and resulted in a new and higher spiritual organic unity—a unity in diversity—that of a humanity which was sanctified by faith in Jesus Christ.[8]

The kingdom of God was no longer hindered by its continual clash with Jewish traditionalism and legalistic influences. No longer would the church be pressured to conform to the Judaistic mold. Following the tragic events surrounding the collapse of Israel's national existence in 70 A.D., the kingdom of God, unshackled by Judaism, was brought into full focus. Indeed, the kingdom of God in its full universal capacity was thrust into the light.

With these thoughts in mind, we see that Luke's unique statement was inserted to convey the glorious truth that the kingdom of God would be fully loosed from the restraints and pressures of the old Jewish order in 70 A.D. The destruction of Jerusalem and the excision of the Jewish nation from the kingdom was one of the most important events that has ever occurred on earth, for it signaled the termination of the old order and contributed to safeguarding the church from the occasion of either continuing in Judaism, or being tainted by its influences.

> It is marked in the most unmistakable way the end of the old dispensation and the complete emancipation of Christianity from the thraldom of Judaism . . . the destruction of the city and the theocracy gave a freedom and universality to the

---

8. Lars P. Qualben, *A History of the Christian Church*, p. 51.

gospel which marks an epoch in the history of Christianity and placed the gradually advancing kingdom of Christ on a firm basis.[9]

Had the Jewish nation not been destroyed, the spiritual concepts of the kingdom of God taught by Christ and the apostles would have been much more difficult to enforce. As long as the old city and temple remained, the true spiritual nature of the kingdom of God would have been clouded by the Jewish concept of a natural and temporal kingdom of God. The destruction of Jerusalem, the center of Judaism, meant that the break with the old dispensation was final and complete. It resulted in great blessings to the entire world, for with the demise of Judaism, the true nature of the kingdom was no longer obscured, and the gospel of grace could be presented to the world in all its intended purity and simplicity.

Questions for Discussion

1. Can you locate any pertinent quotes in current prophetic literature which link the parable of the fig tree to the restored statehood of Israel in 1948? Can you find any quotes which base the timing of the Lord's return within forty years (one generation) of that date?
2. Explain whether this parable is a continuation of what Christ had just spoken of concerning His second coming (Matthew 24:30, 31), or is He simply returning to the original line of thought concerning the predicted events which were to alert "that" generation of the nearness of Jerusalem's destruction?
3. Does it seem reasonable that Christ would stress to His disciples that ". . . *this generation* shall not pass away

---

9. A.H. Newman, *A Manual of Church History,* pp. 118-119.

till all these things be fulfilled" when, as dispensationalists claim, He was actually referring to those events which would not even transpire for two thousand years? Why?

4. If the word *generation* in the fig tree parable does not apply to that generation which witnessed the events of 70 A.D., then what does the word "generation" apply to in Matthew 23:36?

5. Is there a strong link between the phrase "all these things" in Matthew 24:2, and "all these things" in Matthew 24:34? If so, discuss what impact this has upon the timing and application of the fig tree parable.

6. After delivering the fig tree parable, why did Jesus so emphatically assure His disciples that "Heaven and earth shall pass away, but my words shall not pass away" (Matthew 24:35)?

7. Do you agree with the application of Luke 21:31 to the collapse of the Jewish nation in 70 A.D.? Please explain.

NO MAN KNOWETH THE TIME!

Chapter Twenty-One

NO MAN KNOWETH THE TIME!

MATT. 24	MARK 13	LUKE 21
36 But of that day and hour knoweth no *man*, no, not the angels of heaven, but my Father only.	32 But of that day and *that* hour knoweth no man, no, not the angels which are in heaven, neither the Son, but the Father.	

One of the greatest prophetic enigmas facing the church is not, "Will the Lord return?" but, "When will He return?" This question has been asked countless times. Each generation has given rise to those prognosticators who have confidently calculated the timing of Christ's return, and each generation has equally witnessed the privately "inspired" predictions of date-setters dashed upon the rocks of disappointment.

In spite of the many ingenious attempts to ascertain the timing of the second coming, we must raise the fundamental question whether the scriptures provide any information, whatsoever, enabling us to determine the moment of that glorious event. Furthermore, we must ask whether Christ provided any revelations concerning this crucial area of interest. We will now examine one of the most significant prophetic passages in all the Bible to settle this issue.

"But!"

Thus far, the subject of Israel's impending judgment has occupied a place of paramount importance in the Lord's thoughts. Up to this point, the brunt of Christ's prophetic words have predominately centered upon the initial question raised by His disciples concerning the timing of Jerusalem's destruction. He had just concluded the first half of His discourse (Matthew 24:4-35) in relationship to that

206

tragic event with the "fig tree" analogy. In finishing the first division of the prophecy, Jesus left His contemporaries with the sobering reality that Jerusalem's desolation would become historic fact within their generation. He then sealed His words with the absolute assurance that, "Heaven and earth shall pass away, but my words shall not pass away!" (Matthew 24:35). However, beginning with verse 36, a distinct shift is observed in the direction of Christ's prophetic remarks. His attention now focuses upon the secondary questions raised by His followers involving the sign of His coming and the timing of the end of the age.

Matthew 24:36 marks an important juncture in the focus of Christ's prophetic discourse. Some expositors have labeled this passage as the "transition verse" of the prophecy. This section represents a significant turning point in the Olivet prophecy. The obvious transition can be attested to by the word "but" in verse 36, revealing a striking contrast between the subject matter now at hand, and the previous information. There is an abrupt transition from the events bearing directly upon 70 A.D., and those encompassing the end of the age. In responding to the disciples' questions, the Lord now passes from the immediate subject of the judgment upon the Jewish nation, to the more distant subject of His second coming.

An Illuminating Contrast

The insertion of the word "but" not only marks a distinct change in subject matter, it also introduces a vivid contrast between the specific features associated with Jerusalem's desolation and those accompanying the end of the world. As Heffren commented:

We draw attention to the contrast between the vivid and detailed description of the signs given for the followers of Christ to escape the judgment of Israel and the destruction of Jerusalem, and a total lack of specific signs preceding the end of the world.[1]

A perception of this striking contrast will aid the prophetic student immeasurably in attempting to accurately interpret this prophecy, as well as the interpretation of all prophecies related to the end of this present age.

In the first half of the Olivet discourse, Jesus had striven to provide His disciples with specifics concerning the requested sign which was to precede Jerusalem's destruction; however, in the second half of the discourse, the Lord was purposely indefinite and general. In addressing the subject of Jerusalem's impending destruction, the believers were provided complete and unmistakable instructions concerning the signs they were to watch for, and the manner in which to conduct their escape. But in response to the remainder of the disciples' question, namely, "What shall be the sign of thy coming and the end of the world?" Christ declared, "of that day knoweth no man. . . ." This verse opens with the blunt revelation that no extraordinary signs would be given to alert the disciples of the certainty of His approaching advent.

This important contrast between these widely separated events is repeatedly emphasized within the Olivet prophecy. One event was close at hand (Jerusalem's destruction). It would happen within the time span of that generation (40 years), and would be immediately preceded by an obvious sign ("abomination of desolation"). The other event (the second coming), would transpire in the future at a time

---

1. H. C. Heffren, *The Signs of His Coming*, p. 26.

unknown even to the Lord, and would not be preceded by distinguishable signs.

Concerning the first event, He had pointedly stated: "Behold, I have foretold you all things" (Mark 13:23); but concerning the second coming, He left them with only a statement of indefiniteness: "But of that day and hour knoweth no man, no, not the angels which are in heaven, neither the Son, but the Father" (Mark 13:32). In the first section, the disciples are provided an opportunity to flee; however, in the second section involving the timing of the Lord's return, there is no opportunity to flee (Matthew 24:40, 41). Judgment, isolated to the geographic region of Palestine, is the subject of the first section, while the world-wide judgment at Christ's coming is the subject of the second.

Explicit signs were given to alert the believers of Jerusalem's impending destruction. But concerning the second coming, Jesus likened His advent to the unexpected approach of a thief in the night. The obvious implications of this comparison is that no precursory signs will be manifested to herald His coming. Jesus included the parable of the fig tree to remind His disciples that obvious signs would be provided to warn that very generation of the exact timing of Jerusalem's destruction; however, the parable of the "thief in the night" was inserted in stark contrast to inform all believers that the second coming would not be preceded by any preparatory warnings. As William Lane commented,

> While the parable of the fig tree illustrates the possibility of observing the proximity of the first event, another comparison is developed in connection with verse 32 (Mark's account, same as Matthew 24:36) which underscores the impossibility of knowing the moment of the Lord's return.[2]

2. William L. Lane, *The Gospel of Mark*, pp. 481-482.

In the first half of the prophecy, Jesus had clearly stated that Jerusalem's destruction was rapidly approaching and would overtake that very generation of Jews. However, in the second half, the point of indefiniteness and delay is repeatedly stressed concerning the timing of the Lord's return (see Matthew 24:45-51). The factor of indefiniteness is particularly prominent in Matthew's account. For example, in Matthew 24:42 we read: "Watch therefore: for *ye know not* what hour your Lord doth come"; in verse 44 we read: "Therefore be ye also ready: *for in such an hour as ye think not* the Son of man cometh"; in verse 50: "The Lord of that servant shall come in a day when he looketh not for him, and in an hour that he *is not aware of*"; and in chapter 25, verse 13 we read: "Watch therefore, for *ye know neither the day nor the hour* wherein the Son of man cometh." As Philip Mauro states:

> This feature of his coming—its unexpectedness is stated in so many ways, and is so emphatically applied and illustrated that we are absolutely controlled by it in the interpretation, not only of the Mount Olivet discourse, but of every other prophecy relating to the second coming of Christ.[3]

This crucial truth has a significant bearing upon all prophecies related to the second coming, and it is absolutely imperative that the prophetic student grasp it if he ever hopes to arrive at a balanced prophetic perspective concerning the end of the age.

"You Know Not When the Time Is!"

This concept is not foreign to the scriptures or the result of freak exegesis. Many attempt to evade the force of this truth by claiming that it is only the exact "day and hour"

---

3. Philip Mauro, *Seventy Weeks and the Great Tribulation*, pp. 261-262.

which is hidden from our perception. With this exegetical maneuver, they claim that Christ's statement does not forbid us from calculating the precise year of His return. This is not sound exegesis, but "eisegesis" (the reading into a text what is not there). On this point, one author stated that,

> an excellent example of the kind of exegesis that gets one nowhere is the position taken by some that while Jesus said no one knows the day or the hour, He does not say that no one knows the year! That attitude comes very close to handling the Word of God deceitfully. [4]

This tactic does not do interpretive justice to the clarity of Christ's statements, for He obviously intended to convey the great prophetic truth that the timing of His return will be a perpetual matter of uncertainty until it actually transpires. As if to reinforce this point, He added the emphatic insistence in Mark's account:

> . . . watch and pray: FOR YE KNOW NOT WHEN THE TIME IS! (Mark 13:33).

The question of timing is not limited to just the day or hour, but of time in general.

Concerning the general "times" and the particular "seasons," Paul had explicitly stated:

> But of the *times* and the *seasons*, brethren, ye have no need that I write unto you. For yourselves know perfectly that the day of the Lord so cometh as a thief in the night. For when they shall say, Peace and safety; then sudden destruction cometh upon them, as travail upon a woman with child; and they shall not escape (I Thessalonians 5:1-3).

The saints of Thessalonica had no need of knowing the timing of the Lord's coming, simply because they had already

---

4. Ralph Earle, *The Gospel According to Mark*, p. 161.

been instructed in the established fact that the timing of the Lord's return would be as unexpected as the coming of a thief in the night. In that same context, Paul cautioned all Christians to be prepared, watching, and alert at all seasons, lest it overtake us unexpectedly when we may be in a state of spiritual stupor. It is precisely because of the uncertainty of timing that Christians are repeatedly exhorted to remain spiritually alert. The very fact that a distinct air of uncertainty constantly surrounds the actual timing of the second coming is meant to challenge Christians to ever maintain a watchful and expectant attitude lest that day overtake us suddenly, when we are unprepared. Though we will never know for certain the exact time when He will return, we can be sure that we are not caught off-guard when He comes. Our responsibility, then, is not to know the timing of His return, but to be adequately prepared for His return, regardless of the timing.

By recognizing this truth of indefiniteness, we are led to an important and fundamental conclusion: the timing of the second coming and the end of this age will be shrouded in uncertainty until the very moment when it unexpectedly bursts upon the stage of human history. Though this truth is firmly established in the scriptures, the eschatological perspectives underlying the teachings of numerous prophetic interpreters are in direct conflict. Many students of prophecy contend that the timing of the second coming can be known, if not precisely, then at least approximately. However, Christ's simple, straightforward assertion that "no man" would know (know, Greek: eido, to know, be sure of, aware of, perceive, see, understand, tell or know from observation) the time of His advent still holds true.

212

There is no inherent mystery or subtlety regarding this blatant declaration of Jesus, for His words are most transparent. The Lord plainly stated that no man knoweth that day or hour. On this point, G. Campbell Morgan commented:

> . . . there is an arresting insistence upon the fact that the time is not known. . . . In those words (Matthew 24:36) He solemnly warned His disciples, and us, and the whole age, that we know not when, not in this prophecy, nor anywhere else in the teaching of Jesus, not in the whole New Testament is there a single declaration that can help us to fix, even approximately within the limits of human almanac or calendar, the hour of the advent. Nothing could be plainer than this![5]

Regardless of the bold and persistent endeavors of date-setters to pinpoint the precise, or even approximate, timing of the Lord's return, His own words clearly establish the utter impossibility of such attempts, for even Jesus emphasized that it was unknown to Himself (Mark 13:32). If it was unknown to even the "incarnate word of God," then no mere mortal, no matter how prophetically enlightened he may be, will be able to clearly compute the timing of the second coming from his own calculations, natural observations, or from information contained within the Word.

A Blatant Contradiction

How contrary are Christ's teachings to the popularly embraced viewpoint that He will be revealed from heaven at the close of a supposed "Great Tribulation" of determinate length. Contrary to the explicit implications of Christ concerning the absence of distinguishable, preliminary signs

---

5. G. Campbell Morgan, *The Gospel According to Mark*, p. 279.

to herald His return, many expositors are inadvertently challenging His statements by establishing the supposed "Great Tribulation" as a sure sign that His coming is soon at hand. This perspective blatantly contradicts Christ's teachings. No man will be able to determine the timing of the end by the observance of signs. If the condition of the last days will even remotely resemble the common prophetic characterizations of unprecedented, world-wide upheavals, then everyone would know that the end was near.

The fact that there will be no precursory signs to alert the world of the second coming is a biblical truth. Christ included this prophetic point in order to protect God's people from the folly of datesetting and the delusions associated with it. It was inserted to caution the Christian community from presumptuously assuming that every new international crisis, natural catastrophe, or season of natural upheaval was the clear sign of His coming. The inherent wisdom contained in Christ's simple instructions is quite apparent. As H.C. Heffren noted: "Christians are not to look for SIGNS of the coming, but for the Lord himself; they are not waiting for the COMING of the Lord so much as for the LORD who is coming. The emphasis is important. Many go to great lengths trying to predict the future. Each war has produced a host of pseudo-prophets who proclaim Armageddon has arrived and predict the imminent return of the Lord. Several men in each generation claim a revelation of the day of the end of the world; the result has been baneful to the glorious doctrine of the Second Coming and is also in complete defiance of Christ's words that NO man knoweth the day or hour of His return."[6]

---

6. H. C. Heffren, *The Sign of His Coming*, p. 26.

In spite of Christ's clear statement, the church has been repeatedly subjected to the foolish speculations of prophetic forecasters and chart watchers who have presumptuously assured their generation that the second coming would soon arrive. This has been a repeated tendency throughout the breadth of the church age and has frequently had an injurious impact upon the church. Every generation has tended to view the peculiarities of their moment in history as obvious indications of Christ's imminent return and with as justifiable reasons as can be assigned to those today. History has proven them wrong—so what guarantees do we have that our predictions will succeed where so many others have failed?

Every era in the church's history has witnessed Christians who were absolutely convinced that the Lord would soon return, and their conclusions were invariably based upon a private interpretation of the events of their day or a speculative appraisal of the events of tomorrow. But as G. Campbell Morgan so aptly stated: "There has never been an hour in the history of the Christian church, when the signs have not pointed to the possibility of a consummation."[7]

Concerning this point, Boettner commented:

It is a matter of record that wars, national crises, plagues, disasters, earthquakes, etc., invariably have given fresh interest and zeal toward a new reading of the signs of the times and a new outbreak of date-setting. We would observe, however, that these things are not signs of the Second Coming, but events which continue in more or less profusion and in greater or lesser intensity throughout this entire age. There has not been a decade since the time of Christ when they were not in evidence somewhere. At some times they have been more prominent in Europe and America

---

G. Campbell Morgan, *Gospel According to Luke*, p. 238.

and less so in Asia. At other times the reverse has been true. In any event, they have nothing to do with the return of Christ. . . . The fact is that each generation . . . discovers signs which to it are convincing and goes on preaching the same doctrine of the nearness of the end. . . . The signs pointed to forty, or even twenty, years ago have now been forgotten for the most part and remain only in the books and articles written at those times, most of which seem to have been withdrawn as quietly as possible. We may be sure that if the world continues another twenty or forty years, a still different group of signs, at least different in part, will be put forth as evidence that the end is near. [8]

In our day of "prophetic popularity," many are subtly implying, or openly avowing, that this is the very generation that will witness the second coming. Though I am not denying the possibility that the Lord may indeed return before this contemporary generation expires, I do contend that the timing of the Lord's return, ultimately, will never be determined on a basis of construing the signs of the times. Those who counter this assumption have obviously overlooked the plain statements of Christ on this essential point.

Christians are deluged with pamphlets, books, films, tapes, tracts, diagrams and even comic books which essentially claim that the distinctive events of our time are undeniable proofs of Christ's soon return. Often these claims are so dramatized that they smack of prophetic ear-tickling. The grandiose speculations which some expositors have fabricated from a private interpretation of current world events and international trends is little more than empty conjecture. This sensationalized guesswork inevitably fails

---

8. Loraine Boettner, *The Millennium,* pp. 330-331.

to genuinely profit the Christian public. Some prophetic advocates intentionally capitalize upon sensationalizing the events of our present day in an attempt to forcefully prove that they are obvious evidences of the end. Some have boldly gone so far as to predict the actual year of the Lord's return. Though their claims are provocative and intriguing, they are equally misleading and imbalanced, for they are in clear violation of Christ's simple statement:

FOR YE KNOW NOT WHEN THE TIME IS (Mark 13:33).

If this statement was pertinent during Christ's generation, then it will hold equally true throughout all other successive generations—even ours, for His statement was directed to the entire church age. We should earnestly endeavor to heed Christ's caution before presumptuously transgressing the boundaries which He so firmly established concerning the constant state of uncertainty and unexpectancy surrounding the timing of His return. "Christ's wise and balanced statements should strike caution into the most daring exponent of prophecy."[9]

Event-Centered or Christ-Centered?

Many of the end-time imbalances affecting the Christian community are a direct by-product of failing to recognize this basic scriptural perspective. As a result, this error has prompted many to become primarily event-centered in their prophetic outlook. Too often Christians have tended to be more interested in prophetic signs, speculations, and calculations than in considering the balanced instructions of Christ. Tragically, there occasionally has been more of a

9. Alan Cole, *Gospel of Mark*, p. 206.

tendency in laboring to ascertain the timing of the age's end, than in laboring for Christ until the end of the age. The church has been solemnly entrusted with the great responsibility of occupying till He comes (Luke 19:13), rather than being preoccupied with events surrounding His coming. Any prophetic perspective or persuasion which stimulates imbalance in our Christian walk, which needlessly agitates and unsettles our thinking, or negatively affects our labor for the Master is to be regarded with suspicion.

Unfortunately, Christians have too often limited their potential fruitfulness in Christian service because they were absolutely convinced that the Lord would be back in a few years. Because of a failure to grasp the fundamental truth that we have no absolute, infallible guarantee that the Lord will return in our life time, the potential long-range good of the kingdom has needlessly suffered. This error distorts the vision of many believers and causes them to embrace an end-time perspective which prepares for the short haul, rather than the long haul. The biblical attitude of Christians should forever be one of expectancy for the Lord's return, and yet one of constant preparedness in case the Lord may tarry. Christians of every generation should live as if Christ's return is imminent, and yet work and plan as though the present world order will continue indefinitely.

This same error had a detrimental impact upon the Thessalonian Christians during the first century, and Paul moved swiftly to correct it. His wise and timeless admonitions concerning the subject of the timing of the Lord's second coming, and the numerous imbalances in response to it, still apply:

> Now we beseech you, brethren, by the coming of our Lord Jesus Christ, and by our gathering together unto him, *that ye be not soon shaken in mind, or be troubled, neither by*

*spirit, nor by word, nor by letter as from us, as that the day
of Christ is at hand* (II Thessalonians 2:1, 2).

As I have previously pointed out, the obvious implications of these verses are important. The Christian community must always be on guard against any prophetic
persuasion which unsettles the church, fosters fear, or contributes to undermining the work of Christ in the earth. Any
teaching, book, pamphlet, article, or sermon which subtly
weakens our endeavors to *occupy* till He comes should be
cautiously avoided. Any prophetic emphasis which contributes to undermining our state of spiritual preparedness
stands in error. The sensational claims that the Lord's coming is at hand are often responsible for diluting the Christian
resolve to be busy about the Lord's business. The preoccupation with end-time events and timetables has often had a
debilitating impact upon the mission of the church in the
earth. Sadly, some are more enraptured with vain prophetic
timetables and speculative forecasts than in the pressing
spiritual responsibilities which have been entrusted to the
body of Christ.

Christ was no doubt endeavoring to correct such potential
tendencies when He included this statement in His Olivet
prophecy (Matthew 24:36). This statement is exceedingly
practical in its content. "Like every other Christian doctrine,
that of the second coming has a moral goal; it is designed
to promote action more than contemplation. The uncertainty
surrounding the timing was intended to act as a strong stim-
ulant to ceaseless watching rather than appeal to foolish
speculation, curiosity, or an unhealthy devotion to date-
setting."[10] Boettner added:

---

10. *Ibid.*, p. 205.

Since we cannot know the time of Christ's coming, we are to be always ready and always watchful. If men knew that the time of His coming was far off, they would tend to become careless and indifferent about moral and spiritual values. On the other hand, if they knew that the time was very near they would become frenzied and excited and neglect their assigned work. In either event, they would not live normal lives. God prefers that we do not know the time of the end, either the date of our own death, or the end of the world, that our service may be natural, spontaneous, and orderly. He seeks from us that which is the true fruit of our natures, not that which is excited and motivated by the expectation of immediate reward or punishment. This life is for every person primarily a time of testing for character and achievement. But that test could not be carried out with accuracy if our actions were actuated by the hope of immediate rewards of the fear of immediate punishments, or if we were lulled into an attitude of indifference because of knowledge that that accounting was far away. [11]

A Debilitating Influence

The popular belief that the world is presently teetering on the imminent brink of the Great Tribulation has occasionally had an adverse impact upon the work of Christ in the earth. The well-entrenched notion of a "Great Tribulation" period prior to the Lord's return has periodically had a subtle, debilitating influence upon the mission of the church. This prophetic assumption is occasionally responsible for contributing to a spirit of indifference and non-involvement in some quarters of the Christian community. As a direct result,

---

11. Loraine Boettner, *The Millennium*, p. 329.

the Christian resolve to actively respond to the Lord's command to "occupy till I come" (Luke 19:13) has been somewhat stifled. The common belief in an imminent tribulation
period in which Christians will either pass through, or escape altogether by means of a pretribulation rapture, has
frequently produced a spirit of fatalistic resignation. Consequently, some have presumptuously concluded that since
we are so close to the Great Tribulation and Christ's return,
any meaningful efforts to reach the world with the gospel
amounts to little more than an exercise in futility. This fatalistic perspective tends to suppress the fervor underlying
our basic response to the Great Commission, and under-
mines our long-range involvement and commitment to
faithfully engage ourselves in the work of Christ.

A Sign of the End?

In closing, I want to include an additional note concerning the timing of the "Great Tribulation." Many apply it to
the closing seven years of this age immediately prior to the
second coming. In referring to it, Christ had stated that the
obvious sign of the "abomination of desolation" would precede its occurrence. He was very specific concerning the
timing:

> When ye therefore shall see the abomination of desolation,
> spoken of by Daniel the prophet, standing in the holy place,
> (whoso readeth, let him understand:) (Matthew 24:15; see
> also Mark 13:14; and Luke 21:20).

With the manifestation of this clear sign, the disciples would
know with absolute certainty that the predicted period of
great tribulation was about to commence. If this tribulation

221

is referring to the very end of this age, then Christians will obviously know the timing of the Lord's return; they will know that it will be within seven years. But this would directly conflict with the clear statements of Jesus to the contrary: "Ye know not when the time is" (Mark 13:33). If one holds that the sign of the "abomination of desolation" refers to a strict end-time setting, then Jesus hopelessly contradicts Himself, for the appearance of the abomination of desolation would be an indisputable sign of the end. In this case, Matthew 24:15 would be in direct conflict with the plain teaching of Matthew 24:36. If, however, Matthew 24:15 refers to the destruction of Jerusalem in 70 A.D., and Matthew 24:36 refers to the timing of the second coming as I have contended, then there is no conflict and the scriptures are reconciled.

Questions for Discussion

1. Why did Christ state that no man knows the timing of His return in the first place? Why didn't He just remain silent on this issue?
2. Discuss why the Lord would want to come back suddenly and without preparatory warnings.
3. Can you give any notorious examples of date-setting in church history? Can you give any contemporary examples?
4. Discuss why the Lord so emphatically and repeatedly stressed that the timing of His return was unknown.
5. Why does there seem to be such a strong tendency in human nature to relax our efforts or drift into carelessness when we suspect that the Lord's return is imminent?

6. Why does an expectation of the imminent return of Christ tend to dampen evangelistic efforts rather than encourage them?

7. Can you provide any examples where the long-range good of the kingdom has needlessly suffered because of a belief in the soon return of Christ?

8. Dispensationalists claim that there will be many signs prior to the second coming. If this is so, why did Jesus so forcefully state that no one would know the time? Aren't these two perspectives contradictory? Please explain.

9. List any other passages which point out the indefiniteness surrounding the timing of the second coming.

10. As a project, make a comparative list contrasting the points of difference between the first half of the prophecy dealing with Jerusalem's destruction, and the second half dealing with the second coming.

"BUT AS THE DAYS OF NOAH WERE"

Chapter Twenty-Two

"BUT AS THE DAYS OF NOAH WERE"

MATT. 24	MARK 13	LUKE 21
37 But as the days of Noe were, so shall also the coming of the Son of man be. 38 For as in the days that were before the flood they were eating and drinking, marrying and giving in marriage, until the day that Noe entered into the ark, 39 And knew not until the flood came, and took them all away; so shall also the coming of the Son of man be. 40 Then shall two be in the field; the one shall be taken, and the other left. 41 Two *women shall be* grinding at the mill; the one shall be taken, and the other left.		34 And take heed to yourselves, lest at any time your hearts be overcharged with surfeiting, and drunkenness, and cares of this life, and so that day come upon you unawares. 35 For as a snare shall it come on all them that dwell on the face of the whole earth.

Did Christ provide any indications of what the last days would be like? Though He had clearly stressed that no one could determine the timing of His return by observing the "signs of the times," He did not leave the church in total darkness concerning the distinguishing features of those days preceding His advent. However, His brief, but sweeping, portrayal of prevailing world conditions at the moment of His return is in stark contrast to those which are so commonly suggested in prophetic literature. He doesn't paint the grim picture of economic turmoil, global chaos, or natural upheaval—quite the reverse! What, then, will those last days be like?

Christ's Description

Rather than depicting any dramatic features which would tend to alert the world of the imminence of the second coming, the characteristic features of those days will actually tend to contribute to a prevailing sense of uncertainty surrounding that climactic event. Rather than portraying a period of unprecedented global catastrophies, Christ depicts it as a period of relative normalcy. Instead of describing a period keynoted by unparalleled calamities and obvious preliminary portents heralding His imminent return, Jesus clearly reveals that it will be a time when humanity will be thoroughly immersed in the pursuance of the routine affairs of this life. He compares the days preceding the second coming to those of the antediluvian world during the days of Noah:

> For as in the days that were before the flood they were eating and drinking, marrying and giving in marriage, until the day that Noah entered into the ark, and knew not until the flood came . . . so shall also the coming of the Son of man be (Matthew 24:38, 39).

So unexpected will be the actual appearance of the Lord in judgment, in parallel manner to the judgment which was suddenly unleashed upon the antediluvians, that Jesus stated that they:

> . . . KNEW NOT until the flood came and took them all away; SO SHALL ALSO THE COMING OF THE SON OF MAN BE (Matthew 24:39).

His comparison is striking. Rather than predicting a world warned of the nearness of His coming in judgment, the converse is true. Instead of characterizing a world staggering under a devastating series of obvious end-time portents, Jesus depicts a world which will be caught completely off-guard by the very normalcy of the day.

> Jesus makes it clear that there is no means of foretelling the precise events which will usher in the end of the age and

events will be as unforseen and as unexpected as the coming of the flood in the days of Noah. . . . Men and women will be engaged upon their usual occupations, cultivating the fields, grinding corn at the mills, enjoying the conviviality of human fellowship, marrying and giving their children in marriage, when in a moment when He is least expected the Son of man will come.[1]

In Luke's gospel we read an expanded characterization of the last days. Luke further emphasizes the true nature of the days preceding the second coming in the eschatological passages of chapter 17:

Likewise also as it was in the days of Lot; they did eat, they drank, they bought, they sold, they planted, they builded; but the same day that Lot went out of Sodom it rained fire and brimstone from heaven, and destroyed them all. Even thus shall it be in the day when the Son of man is revealed (Luke 17:28-30).

Luke's account further likens the last days to those of Sodom and Gomorrah. The judgment of God suddenly fell at a time when humanity was principally devoted to pursuing a self-indulgent lifestyle. "In both cases, there was nothing to indicate the exact time of judgment until the blow fell with an irretrievably disastrous and exterminating effect. . . . Jesus said it would be like that at the second coming."[2]

Normalcy or Great Tribulation?

In view of Christ's brief description of the days preceding His return, we must ask if it is justified to present the speculative state of affairs which is so popularly envisioned by

---

1. R.V.G. Tasker, *The Gospel According to Matthew*, p. 227.
2. H.C. Heffren, *The Mission of the Messiah*, p. 51.

many. Is it warranted to depict the last days as a period of great tribulation so unequaled in its devastating proportions that it easily dwarfs anything in previous history? If the days immediately preceding Christ's return are going to be marked by unprecedented natural catastrophies, cosmic disturbances, and international calamities, coupled with the successive outpourings of God's concentrated fury for several years, then how could these earth-shaking situations be justly reconciled with Christ's portrayal of the last days? How could He conceivably characterize those days as a time essentially noted for the routine continuance in the mundane affairs of living? How could such normal activities of life, such as depicted by Jesus, possibly co-exist in a world which is reeling under the greatest calamities ever endured by mankind? As Guiness commented:

> If such signs as are imagined by some were to precede the advent, the state of society predicted in these passages (Matthew 24:37-39; Luke 17:26-30) could not by any possibility exist. If monstrous, unheard of, supernatural, portentous events were to transpire, would they not be telegraphed the same day all over a startled world, and produce such a sense of alarm and expectation that buying and selling, planting and building, marrying and giving in marriage, would all be arrested together, and *"Peace and safety"* would be far from anyone's lips or thoughts. . . . No, there was nothing special to alarm the antediluvians before the day that Noah entered into the ark; nothing special to startle the men of Sodom ere the fire from heaven fell; and like as it was in those days, so will it be in these. All going on just as usual, no stupendous sign to attract the world's attention.[3]

---

3. H. Grattan Guiness, *Light For The Last Days*.

In view of this prophetic appraisal, are we safe in concluding that if such catastrophic events as are imagined by many were to transpire at the closing years of this age that men would so lightly ignore the obvious and persist in pursuing the status quo under the false sense of assurance that peace and safety was their secure possesssion? "If all hell will break loose upon the earth in the way some have proclaimed, surely after undergoing this for seven years, people would not be saying, *'peace and safety'* (I Thessalonians 5:3). . . . . And if the literal sun and the literal moon will be darkened just prior to the second coming, would people still be marrying and giving in marriage, planting and building, buying and selling?"[4]

Though there will be scattered international crises, economic fluctuations, and sporadic outbreaks of distress and natural calamities in the earth (the general characteristics of the entire age), the basic state of world affairs will be one of relative normalcy, rather than unprecedented turbulence. Certainly, there will be the typical fluctuations in world affairs, but nothing so drastic as to cause us to stop attending the normal affairs of living. If the reverse was true, as many prognosticators would have us believe, then Christ's own description of the times would carry little weight.

If the actual conditions of the last days are to supposedly be characterized by the cataclysmic events of "The Great Tribulation," coupled with a prolonged period of the outpourings of God's wrath, then we must ask why the Lord didn't clearly say so. Why did He endeavor to suggest a totally different picture to His people? Christ's characterization is diametrically opposed to those which are so

---

4. Ralph Woodrow, Great Prophecies of the Bible, pp. 99-100.

frequently spectacularized and sensationalized by numerous speculators.

The principal features characterizing those days appears to be that of rampant materialism, careless indifference, gross self-indulgence, and the normal pursuance of temporal existence. The picture the Lord paints happens to be one of a thoroughly secularized world going about the routine affairs of life. As Geldenhuys commented:

> As in the time before the Deluge, the great masses of people will, even up to the moment of His advent, be completely engrossed in earthly material and evanescent affairs and will not take heed to be prepared for His coming.[5]

G. Campbell Morgan added:

> Things will be going on just as they were in the days of Noah and Lot. All the ordinary avocations of life on the material plane, eating and drinking, giving in marriage, buying and selling, will be going on, when suddenly, crashing across the common places of life, the Son of man will be manifested. The day of the unveiling of the Son of man will break upon all the world's affairs suddenly. . . . In that day He will find the world going on just as in the days of Noah and Lot.[6]

"Peace and Safety"

Paul's description of the days preceding the second coming are in perfect accord with Christ's Olivet characterization. The apostle states that it will be a period when men will be claiming "peace and safety" (I Thessalonians 5:3). The

---

5. Norval Geldenhuys, *Gospel of Luke*, p. 441.
6. G. Campbell Morgan, *Studies in the Four Gospels, Luke*, p. 201.

implication is that it will be a time when men will be confidently declaring "It is a period of peace and safety." Paul specifically declares that in that day, the Lord will unleash "sudden destruction" upon them at His coming. At a season when men are boldly proclaiming, "Peace and safety," sudden destruction will be unleashed upon the earth. Christ will surprise an unthinking world when He comes the second time. Just as in the days of Noah, when men were busily pursuing their normal vocations or were engaged in social activities, Christ will break in upon the scene and disturb their complacency. Therefore, Christ warned, "be ye also ready for in such an hour as ye think not the Son of man cometh. . . ." The world community will simply not be expecting His coming when He returns.

". . . And So That Day Come Upon You Unawares"

In Luke's Olivet account, Christ carefully warns believers against the potential danger of being overcome by the corruptive influences accompanying those days:

And take heed to yourselves, lest at any time your hearts be overcharged with surfeiting, and drunkenness, and the cares of this life, and so that day come upon you unawares. For as a snare shall it come on all them that dwell on the face of the whole earth (Luke 21:34, 35).

Again, we can safely conclude from Luke's wording that it will be a time highlighted by widespread indifference, materialistic attachment, and a thorough involvement in the earthly affairs of this life. Christ further warns Christians to "take heed to yourselves, lest . . . that day (the day of His coming in judgment) come upon you unawares. For as a snare shall it come on all them that dwell on the face of the whole earth (Luke 21:34, 35). The word which Luke employs for "unawares" is the Greek word *aphnidios*. It is the same word which Paul used in I Thessalonians 5:3 for "sudden." He reveals that the manifestation of the day of the Lord will be "sudden," at a time when men are consumed with a false sense of security.

In Luke 21:36, we are admonished to watch and pray "that we may be accounted worthy to escape all these things . . . and to stand before the Son of man." We are cautioned to remain spiritually awake so that we may insure our escape from "these things"; however, the escape which Christ refers to is not a speculative pre-tribulation rapture prior to a supposed period of great tribulation. The immediate context reveals what these things are in reference to, and how we may safely escape them. "These things" from which we may escape are both the debilitating influences of surfeiting, drunkenness, and the cares of this life, as well as the awesome terrors and wrath which will suddenly consume them who are overcharged with the prevailing influences of those days preceding Christ's return in judgment. Our sole guarantee for successfully weathering the potentially corruptive characteristics of that time will be through the steadfast maintenance of our spiritual vigilance. The coming of Christ will be as unexpected as the sudden springing of a fowler's snare upon "all them that dwell on the face of the whole earth" (Luke 21:35). But it will not be the deadly snare of sudden judgment for those who remain awake. According to the warning of Christ, we must "take heed to ourselves lest at any time our hearts be overcharged (burdened) with surfeiting, drunkenness, and the cares of

232

this life, and so that day come upon you unawares" (Luke 21:34). To them who fail to recognize the true characteristics of the last days as described by Christ, and fail to give serious heed to Christ's exhortation to ceaseless vigilance, the day of the Lord will fall as unexpectantly as God's judgment fell upon Sodom and Gomorrah and the antediluvian world.

The Sin of Sodom

Other scriptural texts also imply that the days preceding the second coming will be marked by a rampant state of carnal security, carelessness, hedonism, gross materialism, and spiritual indifferences, rather than a state of world-wide catastrophies and unparalleled disorders. For example, the prophet Ezekiel further described the prevailing characteristics of the world during the days preceding Sodom's destruction by pinpointing their specific sins:

> Behold, this was the iniquity of thy sister Sodom: pride, fulness of bread, and abundance of idleness was in her and in her daughters, neither did she strengthen the hand of the poor and needy (Ezekiel 16:49).

It was a period when men were proud, satisfied with the fulness of bread, the abundance of idleness, and possessing little concern for others. The implication of Ezekiel's characterization is that it was a day of rampant self-sufficiency (proud), material prosperity and leisure time (fulness of bread and abundance of idleness), and a greater egocentric concern for their own well-being than for others.

Laodicea and the Last Days

Likewise, in Revelation 3:14-22, we read the sobering statements contained in the seventh letter to the church of

Laodicea. The common prophetic position which holds that each letter was penned to a specific period in church history sees the warnings delivered to the Laodicean church in the historic context of the days preceding the Lord's return. If this is an accurate perspective, then we notice that even the church is chided by the Lord for its sense of self-sufficiency, material prosperity, and its presumptuous attitude of carnal security. It is not a picture of a church being challenged, stirred, and purified by the intensities of tribulation and external pressures; it is a tragic portrayal of a church which is desperately in need of severing the cords of affection and affinity to the prevailing influences of their period—a period so fitly depicted by the Lord in His Olivet characterization.

What Do the Scoffers Say?

The implication that, for the most part, business will be continuing as usual until the very moment when the Lord breaks through the heavens, is also seen in the Apostle Peter's comments upon the last days. In II Peter 3:3, 4, we read:

> Knowing this first, that there shall come in the last days scoffers, walking after their own lusts, and saying, Where is the promise of his coming? For since the fathers fell asleep, all things continue as they were from the beginning of the creation.

Rather than suggesting that there will be distinguishable, earth-shaking portents to announce to the world the imminence of the Lord's return, scoffers, absorbed with the prevailing sensuality and self-indulgent spirit of their day, will be demanding where the promise of the Lord's coming is. They will be claiming that "all things continue as they were from the beginning of the creation." The obvious implication, in harmony with their world view, is that things will be generally continuing as they always have. Oh, there will be periodic crises and international disturbances, but these, as we have previously indicated, were to be the general features of the entire age (wars, rumors of wars, earthquakes, famines, pestilences, etc.). But, by the scoffers' own confession, there will not be any of the earth-shaking calamities on the scale that some prophetic speculators have imagined to lead the last day mockers to the opposite conclusion that things are *not now* continuing as they have from the beginning. Peter goes on to declare that in the midst of this prevailing air of scoffing, the Lord will return dramatically and suddenly like a thief in the night, unleashing the awesome judgment of God upon an unsuspecting world (II Peter 3:10).

During the Normal Affairs of Life

Matthew further likens the prevailing conditions of the last days to a time when men will be engaged in the ordinary affairs of secular life until the moment when the great separation between believers and unbelievers transpires at the second coming of Christ:

> Then shall two be in the field; the one shall be taken, and the other left. Two women shall be grinding at the mill; the one shall be taken, and the other left (Matthew 24:40, 41; see also Luke 17:34-37).

These passages imply that mankind will be busily pursuing the normal affairs of living (cultivating their fields, processing their produce, sleeping in the night), until the precise moment when believers will be suddenly taken from the midst of an unbelieving world. The cleavage will be so unsuspecting that men will actually be caught in the middle of their normal daily affairs, just as it was during the days of Noah when men were eating and drinking, buying and selling, planting and building, marrying and giving in marriage, until that very day that Noah entered the ark and the judgment fell. At that moment, believers will be received unto the Lord, and sudden destruction shall fall upon a Godless world, just as God's fiery judgment had fallen suddenly upon Sodom "the *same day* that Lot went out" of the city (Luke 17:29).

Questions for Discussion

1. In your opinion, does Christ's characterization of the last days lend itself to a period of Great Tribulation? Please explain.
2. Why would Jesus characterize the days preceding His return as a time of relative normalcy if, as dispensationalists claim, that period will be marked by unparalleled catastrophies? How could these two conditions co-exist?
3. In reviewing the Genesis accounts in Noah's day and the condition of Sodom and Gomorrah, can you describe any other characteristics of the last days?
4. In I Thessalonians 5:3, Paul reveals that "sudden destruction" shall fall upon the human race at a time when men are proclaiming "peace and safety." What does the phrase "peace and safety" say about the prevailing characteristics of the last days?
5. Discuss the deeper implications of the phrase *surfeiting,*

drunkenness, and the cares of this life mentioned in Luke 21:34.

6. Many dispensationalists claim that Noah is a type of the church being raptured from the earth prior to a Great Tribulation period. How do we reconcile this belief with Christ's revelation that on the same day that Noah entered the ark, the flood came and destroyed all that remained? Furthermore, Christ also stated that "the same day that Lot went out of Sodom, it rained fire and brimstone from heaven, and *destroyed them all.*" If the removal of the church happens on the "same day" as the total destruction of wicked humanity, how can there remain a prolonged period of Great Tribulation?

7. Can you give any examples of modern day scoffers who are denying the second coming?

"WATCH YE THEREFORE"

Chapter Twenty-Three

"WATCH YE THEREFORE"

MATT. 24	MARK 13	LUKE 21

42 Watch therefore: for ye know not what hour your Lord doth come.

43 But know this, that if the goodman of the house had known in what watch the thief would come, he would have watched, and would not have suffered his house to be broken up.

44 Therefore be ye also ready: for in such an hour as ye think not the Son of man cometh.

45 Who then is a faithful and wise servant, whom his lord hath made ruler over his household, to give them meat in due season?

46 Blessed is that servant, whom his lord when he cometh shall find so doing.

47 Verily I say unto you, That he shall make him ruler over all his goods.

48 But and if that evil servant shall say in his heart, My lord delayeth his coming;

49 And shall begin to smite *his* fellowservants, and to eat and drink with the drunken;

50 The lord of that servant shall come in a day when he looketh not for *him*, and in an hour that he is not aware of,

51 And shall cut him asunder, and appoint *him* his portion with the hypocrites: there shall be weeping and gnashing of teeth.

33 Take ye heed, watch and pray: for ye know not when the time is.

34 *For the Son of man is* as a man taking a far journey, who left his house, and gave authority to his servants, and to every man his work, and commanded the porter to watch.

35 Watch ye therefore: for ye know not when the master of the house cometh, at even, or at midnight, or at the cockcrowing, or in the morning:

36 Lest coming suddenly he find you sleeping.

37 And what I say unto you I say unto all, watch.

36 Watch ye therefore, and pray always, that ye may be accounted worthy to escape all these things that shall come to pass, and to stand before the Son of man.

What was the church to do in the face of Christ's prolonged absence? How was she to respond to the challenges of delay, and the perpetual uncertainty surrounding the timing of the second coming? How was she to cope with the unique pressures which this age would produce, as she awaited her Lord's return? And what steps, if any, was she to take to insure her preparation for His eventual appearance? These concerns were at the heart of Christ's final prophetic comments.

"Watch!"

Jesus concludes His prophetic discourse by stressing the constant need for vigilance. The summons to unwavering watchfulness is based fundamentally upon the important insights which He had just provided His followers. He had revealed that the timing of the second coming will be cloaked in uncertainty until the very moment when it suddenly transpires. He had also given a brief sketch of the characteristics highlighting the days preceding His advent. He described it as a period whose prevailing features would actually tend to promote a state of carelessness and indifference, rather than watchfulness and expectancy.

We will now examine the call to watchfulness against the backdrop of both of these crucial points—the factor of uncertainty in timing, and the urgent need for watchfulness in the face of the prevailing conditions of the last days. The fact that His concluding challenge to watch is directly related to both of these previous points is demonstrated by the word "therefore" in His opening statement of this section:

> Watch THEREFORE (for that resason): for ye know not what hour your Lord doth come (Matthew 24:42, see also Mark 13:33 and Luke 21:36).

That is, "Based upon what I have just said, I urge you to conscienciously endeavor to keep awake and watching."

The Missing Links

Christ's repeated exhortations to watchfulness are inseparably linked to the essential fact that the actual moment of His advent remains unknowable, and because it is unknowable, unceasing vigilance is so imperative.

> The duty to watch draws its force from the fact that no one knows the critical moment of God's decisive intervention. . . . It's approach is impossible to discern . . . the day of judgment will arrive so suddenly and unexpectantly that absolutely no one will have the least warning. . . . Because the moment of crisis in unknowable, unceasing vigilance is imperative.[1]

His urgent call to watchfulness is based upon a sober consideration of the prevailing conditions of those days immediately preceding the second coming. In comparing those days to the antediluvian world, the Lord foresaw the potentially debilitating impact that the age of "self-indulgence" would have upon Christendom. His call to watchfulness is exceedingly practical, therefore, in that it alerts all believers of the need for expectancy and alertness due to the uncertainty in timing, as well as cautioning all believers against the subtle danger of losing a sense of vigilance due to the stupifying influences of this age.

Parabolic Parallels

The call to watchfulness is repeatedly emphasized in the Olivet parallels. In Mark's account, the urgency accompanying this exhortation is particularly pronounced. In verse 33 we read "take heed, watch pray . . ."; in verses 34 we observe the brief parable of "the absent householder," in which the porter is commanded to "watch" during the long absence of the master; in verse 35, this truth is applied to

---

1. William L. Lane, *The Gospel of Mark*, pp. 481-483.

each individual: "watch ye therefore"; and in the closing verse of Mark's Olivet account, Christ concludes with the sweeping exhortation: "and what I say unto you [that generation of believers] I say unto all [all successive generations], WATCH!"

This perspective on watchfulness is emphasized in this parallel section of the prophecy through three brief parables: the parable of "the thief in the night" (Matthew 24:43, 44), the parable of "the absent householder" (Mark 13:34-37), and the parable of "the wise and slothful servants" (Matthew 24:45-51). In each parable, the basic theme of watchfulness is viewed from a distinctive vantage point.

In Matthew's parable of "the thief in the night" (see also Luke 12:35-40), the Lord emphasizes the pressing need for constant watchfulness by comparing the uncertainty of the timing of His return to the unsuspecting approach of a thief in the night. The obvious point is that His disciples must not conduct themselves as the unprepared householder who foolishly permitted his house to be broken into because he failed to recognize the reality that thieves do not brazenly advertise beforehand the time of their arrival.

The implication of this poignant parable is that Christians must recognize that the Lord's arrival will not be announced beforehand by obvious preliminary warnings or signs. Therefore, we must always remain spiritually awake, regardless of the hour in the night in which the Lord may choose to come, maintaining a state of alertness so that we will not be unprepared or spiritually asleep when He suddenly returns. As George Ladd wisely commented: "We do not know when the end will come. Therefore, whenever it happens, we must be spiritually awake and must not sleep. If we are awake and Christ comes today, we

242

are ready. If we are awake and Christ does not come until tomorrow, we will still be ready. Whenever it happens, we must be ready."[2]

The Lord capped this parable with the statement that He will actually come at a time when "ye think not the Son of man cometh" (Matthew 24:44). This truth is even more forcefully phrased in Luke's companion parable:

> Be ye therefore ready also: for the Son of man cometh at an hour WHEN YE THINK NOT (Luke 12:40).

These parallel statements clearly imply that the actual timing of the Lord's advent will transpire at a time when believers will tend to assume that it is not the season for His return. As Matthew Henry noted: "Such an hour as the most lively expectants perhaps thought least likely."[3] Rather than appearing at a time preceded by undeniable signs and precursory portents as most men would suppose, the Lord strongly suggests that He will come when men will be assuming it is not the set time for His arrival. In view of this fact, we are admonished to always remain alert, watchful, and ready.

In Mark's parable of "the absent householder," the Lord compares His absence to that of a landholder who takes a far journey:

> For the Son of man is as a man taking a far journey . . . (Mark 13:34).

Before He departed, He left His servants with the commission to remain active and watchful. In this parable, He stresses the factor of indeterminate delay and warns believers of the responsibility of faithfully discharging the duties committed to their trust lest He return unexpectantly and find them sleeping. Though a definite period of delay

---

2. George Ladd, *The Blessed Hope*, p. 115.
3. Matthew Henry, *Matthew Henry's Commentary*, Vol. 5.

is strongly implied in this parable, he cautions His servants to remain continually watching because He could return at any one of the four watches of the night:

> Watch ye therefore: for ye know not when the master of the house cometh, at even, or at midnight, or at the cock-crowing, or in the morning (Mark 13:35).

This parable reveals that the moment of His arrival is un-certain, and that when He does finally return, it will be sudden and unexpected:

> . . . lest coming *suddenly* he find you sleeping (Mark 13:36).

In Matthew's parable of "the wise and slothful servants," Jesus also stresses the factor of delay and uncertainty sur-rounding the actual timing of His return. These points are implied in verses 48 and 50 respectively:

> But and if that evil servant shall say in his heart, My lord *delayeth* his coming. . . . The Lord of that servant shall come in a day when he looketh not for him, and *in an hour he is not aware of* (Matthew 24:48, 50).

These passages clearly suggest the subject of delay through the confession of the evil servant: "my lord delayeth his coming." The subject of uncertainty in timing is further stressed by the assertion that He will return when the servant "looketh not for him, and in an hour he is not aware of."

Watching Is Working

Also contained within the thrust of this parable is the stern warning not only to be faithfully occupied in our labors for Christ, but not to trade upon the apparent delay and emerse ourselves in a life of spiritual irresponsibility and self-in-dulgence (Matthew 24:47-49). Christ enlarges upon the meaning of the word "watch" by strongly implying that one of the fundamental facets underlying the exhortation involves that of spiritual activity, productivity, and business.

This truth is also stressed in Mark's parable of "the absentee landowner" who charged His servants to watch and pray, but also entrusted each of them with realms of stewardship:

> . . . and gave authority to his servants, and to EVERY MAN HIS WORK (Mark 13:34).

In His long absence, His servants were cautioned to watch, pray, and work lest they fall prey to the subtle temptations of carelessness, slothfulness, and self-indulgence. Or as Matthew's parable of "the wise and slothful servant" puts it:

> . . . and shall begin . . . to eat and drink with the drunken (Matthew 24:49).

At the very heart of His commandments to watch is the thought of unceasing spiritual activity. As G. Campbell Morgan stressed: "Watching is working; definite work appointed by the absent Lord; personal work, to each one his work . . . the attitude of the star-gazer with regard to the advent was rebuked at the very beginning of the Christian era when the angel said: 'Ye men of Galilee, why stand ye looking into heaven? This same Jesus . . . shall so come!' . . . our business is to fulfill his command to each his work."[4] The best way that Christ can come upon a man is when he is faithfully, humbly, and watchfully executing his entrusted duty. This is at the heart of Christ's exhortation to watch as well as His command to "occupy (do business) till I come" (Luke 19:13).

A comprehensive understanding of the intended meaning conveyed in the exhortation to watch will aid us in understanding the full scope of Christ's caution. The summons to watch is not a call to fix one's primary interest upon the

---

4. G. Campbell Morgan, *The Gospel According to Mark*, p. 282.

distinctive events of our day, or the speculative events of tomorrow. The repeated exhortations to watch lends absolutely no support to a foolish consumption with end-time speculation and conjecture. It is not a divine endorsement of an event-centered watching, or a challenge to focus our attention upon a constant appraisal of the signs of our day. It is, however, a solemn call to resolutely maintain our undivided loyalty and devotion to our Lord even in the face of delay. It is a call to responsibility, faithfulness, and consistency.

"Be Ye Ready!"

Included within the call to watchfulness is the concept of preparation. The challenge to watchfulness is closely linked to the principle of preparedness. In fact, as William Lane noted: "Vigilance is the responsibility of every believer and provides the sole guarantee of preparedness for the Lord's return."[5]

The subject of preparation is timely whenever we examine the Christian response to the last days. The subject of preparation needs to be stressed whenever we consider the ramifications of last day events and conditions in relationship to the believer's response. In fact, the challenge to "be ye ready" (Matthew 24:44a) is at the center of Christ's prophetic instructions for the church age. The concept of preparedness invariably crops up whenever Christians have undertaken a serious study of the last days, irregardless of their prophetic persuasions. In spite of a wide variety of conflicting eschatological perspectives and theological positions,

---

5. William L. Lane, *The Gospel of Mark*, p. 484.

the principle of preparation is overwhelmingly embraced; however, not all Christians accept like perspectives regarding the subject of preparedness.

Self-Preservation Preparation

In the midst of current prophetic interest, we increasingly hear the latest emphasis involving the subject of preparation. Though the challenge to prepare is a growing watchword in the church, not all that is stressed concerning preparation is necessarily comprehensive or well-balanced.

One of the latest crazes in "prophetic fadism" strongly advocates the concept of "survival preparation" or "self-preservation preparation." This recent slant on the preparation perspective is experiencing an ever-widening popularity, not only among Christians, but unbelievers as well. Both the secular and Christian public is being courted by a growing assortment of books, lectures, and newsletters which fundamentally approach the subject of preparation in the light of the "survival consciousness." It is not uncommon to observe these provocative "do-it-yourself survival guides" in both Christian bookstores or supermarket check-out stands. The basic bottom line thrust of the majority of this new breed of literature stresses the urgent need for comprehensive physical preparation. The urgency surrounding their appeals is invariably based upon their private appraisal of world events, present international trends, or their speculative projections of imminent world-wide calamities.

The Fear Factor

Most of these works blatantly capitalize upon the fear factor in order to forcefully promote their perspective. They

247

often depict a rapidly approaching speculative scenario of coming world events (not necessarily an end-time scenario) of such catastrophic dimensions that the reader is quickly seized by the provocative nature of their perspective. This preparation perspective often builds upon the underlying assumption that nuclear war is inevitable, that unparalleled international disorders are imminent, that unprecedented global monetary crises are looming upon the immediate horizon, that cataclysmic natural phenomena are just around the corner, and so on. Their emphasis on preparation is often based upon little more than a speculative and sensationalized characterization of future events, and the primary appeal for preparation is founded upon the fear of troublesome times.

In view of their studied appraisal of future hard times, we are lectured to invest wisely, purchase dehydrated rations, store water, learn organic gardening, prepare for nuclear hostilities, build bombshelters, and carefully formulate escape routes. We are counseled to invest in gold, silver, money market funds, and T-bills. Some even exhort us to change occupations, consider joining a self-contained Christian communal system, move to a rural setting, or relocated from predicted fall-out zones. These admonitions are echoed both in secular and Christian circles alike.

The primary emphasis of this perspective centers upon the urgent need for natural preparation rather than spiritual readiness. There are a few balanced exceptions, but they are the exception rather than the rule. Some Christian works strongly support the need for practical, commonsense preparation, as well as equally stressing the need for spiritual readiness, and clearly endeavor to maintain a balanced perspective on the theme of Christian preparedness. As one work noted: ". . . for the Christian, self-focused survival planning that in any way overrides commitment to the church and the work of God is dangerous."[6]

Some Christians approach the need for practical preparation from the position that it can actually assist the Christian in times of crisis to be potentially more effective in his service to Christ. If part of the motivating factor for this perspective is predicated upon the assumption that such endeavors can assist the believer in being more productive during times of crisis, then I find little objection, though largely, this is still an unproven assumption. However, most advocates of "survival preparation" place an inordinate emphasis upon the realm of natural preparation only, and the primary motivation for preparing is based upon the fearful expectation of hard times. Often, spiritual considerations are given little or no attention.

A Valid Appeal to Scripture?

Christians who espouse such survivalist sentiments invariably appeal to the scriptures for support. They frequently refer to classic case examples, such as Noah preparing the ark, and Joseph preparing for the seven year famine in Egypt as "proof precedents" of their preparation philosophy.

However, such examples not withstanding, the Lord provided no explicit exhortations concerning the need for "survival preparation" when directly responding to the subject of troublesome times, the last days, or the more immediate subject of Jerusalem's impending destruction. Not once did the Lord admonish His contemporaries to store food rations in the Jordanic mountains for the coming

---

6. Jim Durkin, The Coming World Crisis, pg. 101.

siege of 70 A.D. When touching upon the subject of readiness, the Lord didn't indicate the slightest need for His disciples to engage themselves in survival preparations except to say:

> Then let them which be in Judea flee into the mountains: let him which is on the housetop NOT COME DOWN TO TAKE ANY THING OUT OF HIS HOUSE: neither let him which is in the field return back to take his clothes (Matthew 24:16-18).

Absolutely nothing is given concerning the necessity for developing survival techniques. The only thing that He said concerning the need for prior preparation was:

> PRAY . . . that your flight be not in the winter, neither on the sabbath (Matthew 24:20).

It is my conviction that had Jesus intended for the Christian community to diligently prepare in the manner in which some survival literature would direct us, then He would at least have hinted at it. The primary theme which the Lord repeatedly hammered upon was the constant need for ceaseless vigilance, spiritual alertness, and consistent diligence in well-doing until He comes. This essential emphasis was, and will always be, the ultimate guarantee for adequate Christian preparation.

Not a Scriptural Priority

I should clarify the fact that I am not unequivocally taking issue with the potential wisdom and prudence involved with taking basic, commonsense steps towards physical preparation whether hard times or good times lay ahead. But I do take strong issue with what I feel to be serious imbalances and inherent dangers contained in any emphasis whose preparation focus is primarily physical. There is potentially a subtle error in predominantly focusing the believer's attention upon areas of preparation outside the bounds of those clearly emphasized by the Lord. In a parallel vein with Paul's statement that "Bodily exercise profiteth little; but godliness is profitable unto all things" (I Timothy 4:8), I hold that physical preparation, only, may indeed have a little profit, but striving to spiritually prepare ourselves is far more beneficial.

Again, I do not seek to oppose the constant need and responsibility of exercising the sound biblical principles of wise financial stewardship, resourcefulness, thriftiness, foresight, and prudence; but, ultimately, I recognize that we may run the risk of being thoroughly prepared physically, and just as equally unprepared spiritually. The Lord explicitly and repeatedly admonished the church of all generations to "Take ye heed, watch and pray" (Mark 13:33), and not "Take ye heed, invest and horde."

When viewed against the backdrop of Christ's warnings to watchfulness and prayer, the need for surivival preparation is more a preference and luxury than a scriptural necessity, especially in affluent America. The world community of believers has a far more pressing need for spiritual revival than physical survival. I have no "bones to pick" with those brethren who sincerely see the need for Christians to take prudent, sensible, well-balanced steps towards practical preparation. But I do contend that unless the church diligently strives to maintain a vital state of spiritual readiness and fervency of spirit (see Luke 12:35), while busily occupying herself with the work entrusted to her charge, then all our devotion to material and physical preparation will be less than in vain. The church must consistently guard herself against any persuasion, distraction, or emphasis which would draw our attention away from the fundamental necessity of preparing ourselves spiritually.

The Motivation Factor

I want to address the "motivation factor" underlying our need to prepare. For many believers, the sole incentive for preparation is based upon the expectation of troublesome times. Many view the challenge to prepare against the strict backdrop of coming end-time distresses. The Christian's primary motive for preparing is often only based upon the assumption that grievous tribulation is ahead. However, Christ never intended for hard times to be the exclusive catalyst for promoting the need for preparation. The compelling motivation for preparation must not be based fundamentally upon a fear of things to come. Our duty to watch and pray does not draw its essential force from the possibility that difficult times may lay on our immediate horizon. Christians have been solemnly charged to be ready at all seasons, regardless of future events. Christ intended for the preparation principle to be an abiding rule in the believer's walk whether we face times of distress or times of ease, whether we face hard times or good times, whether we face times of deprivation and poverty, or times of plenty and affluence.

The ultimate concern for believers today involves the pressing need of embracing a comprehensive approach to preparation, regardless of the conditions of the days before us. Irrespective of the possibility of fluctuations in the economy, or the increasing instability among nations, or the rise of international crises, the basic fundamental thrust

undergirding the biblical concept of preparation rests fundamentally upon the subject of spiritual readiness—in devoting the focus of our attention upon being a faithful steward,
in cultivating a vital personal relationship with Christ, in
developing a healthy devotional life, in watching expectantly
for the Lord's return, in walking circumspectly before Him,
in seeking first the kingdom of God and His righteousness,
in winning souls for Christ, and in diligently occupying until
He comes.

Often a balanced Christian perspective on preparation is
being subtly distorted by the popular preoccupation with
the belief that the final days preceding the second coming
will be highlighted by a period of unprecedented calamities
known as "The Great Tribulation." As a direct result, many
are failing to discern the true conditions of the times and
seasons for which they are called to prepare. A lack of
thorough preparedness is often the by-product of failing to
perceive the actual conditions of the last days as characterized by Christ Himself. In view of the prevailing conditions
which Jesus depicted of the days preceding His advent
(see Chapter 22), we have an urgent need to get our over-
all preparation perspective in balance.

The Real and Present Peril

The whole subject of end-time readiness is being partially
obscured by the popular emphasis upon the envisioned
emergence of unparalleled global catastrophies and chaos
during the closing years of this age. Several typical re-
sponses have been adopted in reaction to this end-time
perspective: some are taking serious steps to physically
prepare for the coming troubles; multitudes are conveniently

circumventing a genuine preparation response in the face of a supposed outbreak of last day tribulation by setting their wistful hopes on a pre-tribulation rapture; some are essentially procrastinating, holding in check the serious need for preparation until the actual commencement of certain events; and some are making no preparation attempts at all. On the bottom line, the overwhelming preparation perspective of most Christians is based upon either being ready to endure a "Great Tribulation" period, or upon escaping it all together. However, I feel that this common characterization of the end-time conditions is inadvertently misleading the Christian community from the real dangers threatening our potential state of readiness, and is drawing attention away from the true issues at hand.

In view of Christ's personal description of the days preceding His coming, it would appear not to be so much a time of earth-shattering chaos, but a time of relative normalcy with humanity eating and drinking, marrying and giving in marriage, buying and selling, building and planting, etc. What Christians are explicitly warned to be prepared against is the prevailing conditions of surfeiting, drunkenness, and the cares of this life (Luke 21:34). We are specifically cautioned against becoming entangled and overcharged with the business of living to the extent that we are caught off-guard at His coming.

The real and present peril facing the church is not so much the external threat of tribulation, persecution, wars, rumors of wars, famines, deprivation, or natural calamities, but a far more insidious and potentially debilitating peril, whose very danger lies in the fact that it is so easily imperceived and overlooked. The peril of the days which Christ depicts lies not in its obviousness, but in its subtlety. The actual peril which the Lord clearly implied is not that which is envisioned by numerous prophetic expositors. The pressing threat which challenges the last day church in particular is not the pressures of hard times, tribulations, persecutions, and chaos. It is the danger of self-indulgence, prosperity, materialism, idleness, lukewarmness, carelessness, and indifference.

In spite of the last day predictions of financial prophets, (no pun intended) survival experts, secular soothsayers, or Christian prognosticators, none can alter the Lord's own characterization of those days. It is precisely in view of the prevailing conditions of ease, self-indulgence, and apathy that He repeatedly warned His followers to be spiritually prepared—watching, praying, and laboring at all seasons. They were to recognize the real threat facing them. It would not be primarily that of external tribulation, but the corrosive influences of normalcy and complacency.

The Last Great Test

Historically, the church has faced three essential tests: the test of persecution, the test of poverty, and the test of prosperity. Invariably, she has fared exceptionally well in the face of persecution and poverty. Even in the chronicle of the early church recorded in Acts, the church consistently triumphed over these two trials. Historically, the pressures arising from persecution and poverty have actually served as a beneficial catalyst to stimulate spiritual growth, purity, dedication, and evangelistic expansion in the church. The fires of persecution have often worked to kindle the flames of evangelism and outreach. The church has rarely suffered spiritually under the trials of tribulation. Instead, she has profited and thrived. In some sense, the periodic outbreak of persecution and poverty has served as a god-send for the church. As a rule, the church has prospered during those historic periods of poverty and persecution.

However, the test of prosperity and affluence has often had just the opposite impact. This has been, and is, the most potentially dangerous and devastating test which the church must face, and it is precisely this test which the last day church must primarily endure. The "perilous times" which the church must be prepared for is the peril arising from a self-indulgent age, when "men shall be lovers of their own selves . . . lovers of pleasures more than lovers of God; having a form of godliness, but denying the power thereof" (II Timothy 3:1-5). The subtle perils arising from materialism, affluence, and good times are potentially more debilitating to the people of God than the obvious pressures of persecution and deprivation.

When believers lock their end-time focus upon the trials of persecution and poverty as the real dangers facing the church, they are failing to recognize a far more insidious peril. The church needs to wake up and perceive the clear and present danger facing it. In the process of fixing our eyes upon the speculative events of tomorrow, we are running the risk of failing to properly perceive the perils of today.

The potentially corruptive influences of a materialistic age, consumed with the cares of this life, thoroughly immersed in the business of living—eating, drinking, marrying, giving in marriage, buying, selling, planting, and building was the threat to which Jesus referred. It is this test that can wreak the most havoc upon the Christian community. It is during the test of ease, affluence, and normalcy that the church runs the greater risk of falling prey to self-indulgence, indifference, laxity, and lukewarmness.

Often, without the external pressures of tribulation, the church sinks into a quagmire of apathy and carelessness. Though on the surface, the church may be progressing physically and materially, she may be weak and anemic—little more than the Laodicean church who boasted that she was "rich, and increased with goods, and had need of nothing," when in reality she knew not that she was "wretched, and miserable, and poor, and blind, and naked" (Revelation 3:17).

We have been challenged to be prepared not just for the possible emergence of tribulations, financial crises, or physical deprivation, but for the test of prosperity, plenty, and fulness. This was the obvious test which the Lord hinted at in His general characterization of the last days, and regarding this test, He specifically warned all Christians, especially those at the end, to "take heed lest" (Luke 21:34) the vital life force of their experience be sapped by the prevailing spirit of this age.

We must each awake and be alerted to the real threat which is now at hand; let us be prepared for all eventualities, whether they be good or bad; let us not be side-tracked by the ever-changing currents in the international scene, by unpredictable social trends, by economic fluctuations, or by prophetic speculations. The eyes of the church, corporate and individual, are to be single, focused upon the Great Commission of reaching a lost world for Christ, of ever establishing the stability and strength of the kingdom of God, of redeeming the time before us, of ever remaining alert—watching and waiting for the blessed hope of His return!

257

Questions for Discussion

1. As a project, discuss what your response would be if you knew the Lord was returning today. What would your reaction be if you knew the Lord would return in one year? What does this say about our present attitude and response to the Lord's coming?
2. Does Christ's exhortation to watch contain any evidence which suggests an event-centered watching, or give support to a watching for signs? Please explain.
3. List other New Testament passages which exhort the church to remain vigilant in light of the Lord's return.
4. In context of the Lord's eventual return, the disciples were told not to stand gazing into the heavens (Acts 1:11). What are the deeper implications of this exhortation for the church today? Has this been a common tendency among Christains? If so, why?
5. Those who embrace a pre-tribulation rapture theory claim that New Testament passages likening the Lord's return to a "thief in the night" support the concept of a secret, silent rapture. Was this what Christ was implying by the illustration of a thief? What other passages compare the Lord's return to a thief in the night?
6. Discuss the inherent weaknesses in a self-preservation consciousness.
7. Should the threat of hard times be the primary motivation for preparation? Please explain. What should be the motivation factor underlying the Christian's responsibility to prepare?
8. Why is the test of prosperity a far more potentially dangerous challenge for the church than the test of poverty or persecution?

9. Do you agree with the statement that the real and present peril confronting the church is not the threat of external tribulation, but the internal threat of carelessness, indifference, and self-indulgence? Why?

10. Why has the periodic outbreak of persecution and poverty served as a "blessing in disguise" for Christendom?

11. Can you find any biblical examples where spiritual or material prosperity has contributed to the downfall of God's people?

12. In II Timothy 3:1, Paul reveals that "in the last days perilous times shall come." What are the specific characteristics he gives of those days? Do perilous times always have to involve external tribulations? Please explain.

13. What important lesson should today's church glean from the example of the Laodicean church?

14. Discuss the single most important perspective or conclusion you gained from this book.

Conclusion

In closing, I recognize that the eschatological perspectives advanced within this book repeatedly challenge the prophetic opinions cherished by many; however, I do not wish to leave anyone with the subtle impression that this work is casting a negative reflection upon the integrity, sincerity, or spiritual competence of those believers who may disagree with the prophetic positions I have taken. Though I have endeavored to reasonably and scripturally enforce the prophetic viewpoints contained within this exposition, I sincerely pray that the polemic style occasionally employed has not seemed unduly abrasive. In view of the potential clash of eschatological opinions involving the material presented in this work, I earnestly appeal to each reader to thoughtfully consider the following words.

Though Christians may stand firmly together "striving for the faith of the gospel" and earnestly defending the essential tenets of the Christian faith, the speculative quality of prophetic interpretation has been, and continues to be, the grounds of contention, confusion, and dogmatism between earnest believers of differing persuasions. Though we must be unyielding, unbending, and uncompromising concerning the essentials of our faith, we must always exercise an attitude of tolerance towards those brethren who may disagree with our prophetic positions.

The highly speculative nature of prophetic interpretation, coupled with a myriad of conflicting viewpoints, presents Christianity with a potentially volatile area of disagreement and confrontation. This potential for disagreement and discord presents a serious challenge to every believer in striving to maintain the essential balance of peace with those who may earnestly disagree with us concerning our private prophetic positions.

Our differences should never cause us to malign the sincerity or genuineness of those who do not side with our opinions. Our essential unity and fellowship in Christ should never be severed or undermined because of our differences on prophetic points. Our eschatological differences should never be made a ground of fellowship, a test of orthodoxy, or a necessary element in Christian doctrine. We must faithfully exercise the spirit of liberty and charity towards opposing viewpoints. As the old maxim goes, "In essentials unity, in non-essentials liberty, in all things charity." If we must disagree with one another in defending our prophetic opinions—we must agree to disagree—agreeably.

In the final analysis, our prophetic appraisals must always be tempered by that wisdom which is from above, which is pure, peaceable, gentle, easy to be entreated, full of mercy and good fruits, without partiality, and without hypocrisy (James 3:17). In spite of whatever divergence of opinion we may possess concerning our private prophetic positions, may we all continue striving together in the faith of the gospel, looking for, hasting unto, and loving His appearing.

THE MT. OLIVET PROPHECY IN PARALLEL

MATT. 24

And Jesus went out, and departed from the temple: and his disciples came to him for to shew him the buildings of the temple.

2 And Jesus said unto them, See ye not all these things? verily I say unto you, There shall not be left here one stone upon another, that shall not be thrown down.

3 And as he sat upon the mount of Olives, the disciples came unto him privately, saying, Tell us, when shall these things be? and what shall be the sign of thy coming, and of the end of the world?

4 And Jesus answered and said unto them, Take heed that no man deceive you.

5 For many shall come in my name, saying, I am Christ; and shall deceive many.

MARK 13

And as he went out of the temple, one of his disciples saith unto him, Master, see what manner of stones and what buildings are here!

2 And Jesus answering said unto him, Seest thou these great buildings? there shall not be left one stone upon another, that shall not be thrown down.

3 And as he sat upon the mount of Olives over against the temple, Peter and James and John and Andrew asked him privately,

4 Tell us, when shall these things be? and what shall be the sign when all these things shall be fulfilled?

5 And Jesus answering them began to say, Take heed lest any man deceive you:

6 For many shall come in my name, saying, I am Christ; and shall deceive many.

LUKE 21

And he looked up, and saw the rich men casting their gifts into the treasury.

2 And he saw also a certain poor widow casting in thither two mites.

3 And he said, Of a truth I say unto you, that this poor widow hath cast in more than they all:

4 For all these have of their abundance cast in unto the offerings of God: but she of her penury hath cast in all the living that she had.

5 And as some spake of the temple, how it was adorned with goodly stones and gifts, he said,

6 As for these things which ye behold, the days will come, in the which there shall not be left one stone upon another, that shall not be thrown down.

7 And they asked him, saying, Master, but when shall these things be? and what sign will there be when these things shall come to pass?

8 And he said, Take heed that ye be not deceived: for many shall come in my name, saying, I am Christ; and the time draweth near: go ye not therefore after them.

MATT. 24

6 And ye shall hear of wars and rumours of wars: see that ye be not troubled: for all these things must come to pass, but the end is not yet.

7 For nation shall rise against nation, and kingdom against kingdom: and there shall be famines, and pestilences, and earthquakes, in divers places.

8 All these are the beginning of sorrows.

9 Then shall they deliver you up to be afflicted, and shall kill you: and ye shall be hated of all nations for my name's sake.

10 And then shall many be offended, and shall betray one another, and shall hate one another.

11 And many false prophets shall rise, and shall deceive many.

12 And because iniquity shall abound, the love of many shall wax cold.

13 But he that shall endure unto the end, the same shall be saved.

14 And this gospel of the kingdom shall be preached in all the world for a witness unto all nations; and then shall the end come.

MARK 13

7 And when ye shall hear of wars and rumours of wars, be ye not troubled: for such things must needs be; but the end shall not be yet.

8 For nation shall rise against nation, and kingdom against kingdom: and there shall be earthquakes in divers places, and there shall be famines and troubles: these are the beginnings of sorrows.

9 But take heed to yourselves: for they shall deliver you up to councils; and in the synagogues ye shall be beaten: and ye shall be brought before rulers and kings for my sake, for a testimony against them.

10 And the gospel must first be published among all nations.

11 But when they shall lead you, and deliver you up, take no thought beforehand what ye shall speak, neither do ye premeditate: but whatsoever shall be given you in that hour, that speak ye: for it is not ye that speak, but the Holy Ghost.

12 Now the brother shall betray the brother to death, and the father the son; and children shall rise up against their parents, and shall cause them to be put to death.

13 And ye shall be hated of all men for my name's sake: but he that shall endure unto the end, the same shall be saved.

LUKE 21

9 But when ye shall hear of wars and commotions, be not terrified: for these things must first come to pass; but the end is not by and by.

10 Then said he unto them, Nation shall rise against nation, and kingdom against kingdom:

11 And great earthquakes shall be in divers places, and famines, and pestilences; and fearful sights and great signs shall there be from heaven.

12 But before all these, they shall lay their hands on you, and persecute you, delivering you up to the synagogues, and into prisons, being brought before kings and rulers for my name's sake.

13 And it shall turn to you for a testimony.

14 Settle it therefore in your hearts, not to meditate before what ye shall answer:

15 For I will give you a mouth and wisdom, which all your adversaries shall not be able to gainsay nor resist.

16 And ye shall be betrayed both by parents, and brethren, and kinsfolks, and friends; and some of you shall they cause to be put to death.

17 And ye shall be hated of all men for my name's sake.

18 But there shall not an hair of your head perish.

19 In your patience possess ye your souls.

MATT. 24

15 When ye therefore shall see the abomination of desolation, spoken of by Daniel the prophet, stand in the holy place, (whoso readeth, let him understand:)

16 Then let them which be in Judaea flee into the mountains:

17 Let him which is on the housetop not come down to take any thing out of his house:

18 Neither let him which is in the field return back to take his clothes.

19 And woe unto them that are with child, and to them that give suck in those days!

20 But pray ye that your flight be not in the winter, neither on the sabbath day:

21 For then shall be great tribulation, such as was not since the beginning of the world to this time, no, nor ever shall be.

22 And except those days should be shortened, there should no flesh be saved: but for the elect's sake those days shall be shortened.

23 Then if any man shall say unto you, Lo, here is Christ, or there; believe it not.

24 For there shall arise false Christs, and false prophets, and shall shew great signs and wonders; insomuch that, if it were possible, they shall deceive the very elect.

MARK 13

14 But when ye shall see the abomination of desolation, spoken of by Daniel the prophet, standing where it ought not, (let him that readeth understand,) then let them that be in Judaea flee to the mountains:

15 And let him that is on the housetop not go down into the house, neither enter therein, to take any thing out of his house:

16 And let him that is in the field not turn back again for to take up his garment.

17 But woe to them that are with child, and to them that give suck in those days!

18 And pray ye that your flight be not in the winter.

19 For in those days shall be affliction, such as was not from the beginning of the creation which God created unto this time, neither shall be.

20 And except that the Lord had shortened those days, no flesh should be saved: but for the elect's sake, whom he hath chosen, he hath shortened the days.

21 And then if any man shall say to you, Lo, here is Christ; or, lo, he is there; believe him not:

22 For false Christs and false prophets shall rise, and shall shew signs and wonders, to seduce, if it were possible, even the elect.

LUKE 21

20 And when ye shall see Jerusalem compassed with armies, then know that the desolation thereof is nigh.

21 Then let them which are in Judaea flee to the mountains; and let them which are in the midst of it depart out; and let not them that are in the countries enter thereinto.

22 For these be the days of vengeance, that all things which are written may be fulfilled.

23 But woe unto them that are with child, and to them that give suck, in those days! for there shall be great distress in the land, and wrath upon this people.

24 And they shall fall by the edge of the sword, and shall be led away captive into all nations: and Jerusalem shall be trodden down of the Gentiles, until the times of Gentiles be fulfilled.

25 And there shall be signs in the sun, and in the moon, and in the stars; and upon the earth distress of nations, with perplexity; the sea and the waves roaring;

26 Men's hearts failing them for fear, and for looking after these things which are coming on the earth: for the powers of heaven shall be shaken.

27 And then shall they see the Son of man coming in a cloud with power and great glory.

28 And when these things begin to come to pass, then look up, and lift up your heads: for your redemption draweth nigh.

29 And he spake to them a parable; Behold the fig tree, and all the trees;

30 When they now shoot forth, ye see and know of your own selves that summer is now nigh at hand.

31 So likewise ye, when ye see these things come to pass, know ye that the king-

23 But take ye heed: behold, I have foretold you all things.

24 But in those days, after that tribulation, the sun shall be darkened, and the moon shall not give her light.

25 And the stars of heaven shall fall, and the powers that are in heaven shall be shaken.

26 And then shall they see the Son of man coming in the clouds with great power and glory.

27 And then shall he send his angels, and shall gather together his elect from the four winds, from the uttermost part of the earth to the uttermost part of heaven.

28 Now learn a parable of the fig tree; When her branch is yet tender, and putteth forth leaves, ye know that summer is near:

29 So ye in like manner, when ye shall see these things come to pass, know that it is nigh, even at the doors.

30 Verily I say unto you, that this gen-

25 Behold, I have told you before.

26 Wherefore if they shall say unto you, Behold, he is in the desert; go not forth: behold, he is in the secret chamber; believe it not.

27 For as the lightning cometh out of the east, and shineth even unto the west; so shall also the coming of the Son of man be.

28 For wheresoever the carcase is, there will the eagles be gathered together.

29 Immediately after the tribulation of those days shall the sun be darkened, and the moon shall not give her light, and the stars shall fall from heaven, and the powers of the heavens shall be shaken:

30 And then shall appear the sign of the Son of man in heaven: and then shall all the tribes of the earth mourn, and they shall see the Son of man coming in the clouds of heaven with power and great glory.

31 And he shall send his angels with a great sound of a trumpet, and they shall gather together his elect from the four winds, from one end of heaven to the other.

32 Now learn a parable of the fig tree; When his branch is yet tender, and putteth forth leaves, ye know that summer is nigh:

33 So likewise ye, when ye shall see all these things, know that it is near, even at the doors.

34 Verily I say unto you, This generation

265

shall not pass, till all these things be fulfilled.

35 Heaven and earth shall pass away, but my words shall not pass away.

36 But of that day and hour knoweth no man, no, not the angels of heaven, but my Father only.

37 But as the days of Noe were, so shall also the coming of the Son of man be.

38 For as in the days that were before the flood they were eating and drinking, marrying and giving in marriage, until the day that Noe entered into the ark.

39 And knew not until the flood came, and took them all away; so shall also the coming of the Son of man be.

40 Then shall two be in the field; the one shall be taken, and the other left.

41 Two women shall be grinding at the mill; the one shall be taken, and the other left.

42 Watch therefore: for ye know not what hour your Lord doth come.

43 But know this, that if the goodman of the house had known in what watch the thief would come, he would have watched, and would not have suffered his house to be broken up.

44 Therefore be ye also ready: for in such an hour as ye think not the Son of man cometh.

eration shall not pass, till all these things be done.

31 Heaven and earth shall pass away: but my words shall not pass away.

32 But of that day and that hour knoweth no man, no, not the angels which are in heaven, neither the Son, but the Father.

33 Take ye heed, watch and pray: for ye know not when the time is.

34 For the Son of man is as a man taking a far journey, who left his house, and gave authority to his servants, and to every man his work, and commanded the porter to watch.

35 Watch ye therefore: for ye know not when the master of the house cometh, at even, or at midnight, or at the cockcrow-

dom of God is nigh at hand.

32 Verily I say unto you, This generation shall not pass away, till all be fulfilled.

33 Heaven and earth shall pass away: but my words shall not pass away.

34 And take heed to yourselves, lest at any time your hearts be overcharged with surfeiting, and drunkenness, and cares of this life, and so that day come upon you unawares.

35 For as a snare shall it come on all them that dwell on the face of the whole earth.

36 Watch ye therefore, and pray always, that ye may be accounted worthy to escape all these things that shall come to pass, and to stand before the Son of man.

MARK 13

ing, or in the morning:

36 Lest coming suddenly he find you sleeping.

37 And what I say unto you I say unto all, Watch.

MATT. 24

45 Who then is a faithful and wise servant, whom his lord hath made ruler over his household, to give them meat in due season?

46 Blessed is that servant, whom his lord when he cometh shall find so doing.

47 Verily I say unto you, That he shall make him ruler over all his goods.

48 But and if that evil servant shall say in his heart, My lord delayeth his coming;

49 And shall begin to smite his fellowservants, and to eat and drink with the drunken;

50 The lord of that servant shall come in a day when he looketh not for him, and in an hour that he is not aware of,

51 And shall cut him asunder, and appoint him his portion with the hypocrites: there shall be weeping and gnashing of teeth.

267

Select Bibliography

The serious student of eschatology will soon discover that the Mt. Olivet discourse is often neglected in prophetic literature. Little comprehensive study has been devoted to this prophecy. Most material in print is written with a strong dispensational bias. However, even a survey of dispensationalist works point up an amazing lack of research into this great prophecy.

To assist the prophetic student, I have included, in the order of significance, only those reference books and commentaries which I consider to be commendable aids to further research. I have omitted hyper-dispensationalist works, though many are included in the General Bibliography. Though some of the commentaries listed have traces of dispensational teachings, they include random information which I found helpful. An endorsement of the following works does not imply complete compatibility with the views expressed in this book.

REFERENCE WORKS:

Seventy Weeks and the Great Tribulation. Philip Mauro; Reiner Pub., Swengel, Penn.

Offers a comprehensive inciseful treatment of the Olivet prophecy in parallel, as well as a thorough examination of Daniel's companion prophecies. I consider this work to be a classic in its field (273 pages).

An Eschatology of Victory. J. Marcellus Kik, Presbyterian and Reformed Publishing Co., Phillipsburg, N. J., 1971.

Offers an excellent exposition of the Olivet prophecy; however, this book may be hard to locate (278 pages).

Great Prophecies of the Bible. Ralph Woodrow, P. O. Box 124, Riverside, Calif. 92502, 1971.

Presents a detailed treatment of the Olivet prophecy in parallel along with tackling such crucial subjects as the rapture, the anti-christ, and Daniel's prophecies. I found this work to be extremely helpful (200 pages).

The Millennium. Loraine Boettner, The Presbyterian and Reformed Publishing Co., Phillipsburg, N. J., 1984, Revised Edition.

Offers an excellent coverage of the Great Tribulation, as well as a host of crucial eschatological topics having a direct bearing upon the Olivet prophecy. His insights into the implications of prophetic positions are particularly enlightening. I highly recommend this work (415 pages).

The Life and Times of Jesus the Messiah. Alfred Edersheim, Eerdmans, Grand Rapids, Mich., 1968.

Extremely helpful insights into the context of the Olivet prophecy (1491 pages).

Josephus. Translated by William Whiston, Baker Book House, Grand Rapids, Mich.

Classic eyewitness accounts serve as an indispensable research tool for those examining the tragic events associated with Israel's destruction in 70 A.D. (4 vols.).

The Sign of His Coming. H. C. Heffren, Bible Truth Depot, Swengel, Penn., 1945.

Covers a wide range of prophetic subjects including a concise but informative appraisal of the Olivet prophecy (64 pages).

The Mission of the Messiah. H.C. Heffren, Bible Truth Depot, Swengel, Penn., 1944.

Offers a limited, but useful, treatment of portions of the Olivet prophecy (64 pages).

The Latter Days. Russell Bradley Jones, Baker Book House, Grand Rapids, Mich., 1961.

Offers helpful insights into the closing events of this age (176 pages).

The Christ of the Gospels. J.S. Shepard, Eerdmans, Grand Rapids, Mich., 1939.

Gives a few constructive insights into the Olivet prophecy (635 pages).

The Hope of Israel. Philip Mauro, Reiner Pub., Swengel, Penn., 1970.

Offers an exhaustive treatment of Israel's place in prophecy. Provides helpful insights into the "times of the Gentiles" (261 pages).

The Kingdom of God. H.M. Riggle, Faith Pub. House, Guthrie, Okla., 1899.

Hard to find and somewhat dated, but gives some useful insights into the prevailing conditions of the last days in accordance with Christ's Olivet predictions (166 pages).

Inspired Principles of Prophetic Interpretation. John Wilmot, Reiner Pub., Swengel, Penn., 1967.

Tackles a variety of prophetic subjects which impact upon the Olivet prophecy (290 pages).

COMMENTARIES:

The Gospel of Luke. Paul T. Butler, College Press, Joplin, Mo., 1981.

Offers a concise and informative exposition of the Olivet prophecy. Recommended for those desiring a brief overview (617 pages).

Clarke's Commentary, Vol. 5. Adam Clarke, Abingdon Press, Nashville, Tenn.

Somewhat dated, but gives a very useful appraisal of the Olivet prophecy (906 pages).

The Gospel According to St. Matthew. R.V. G. Tasker, Eerdmans, Grand Rapids, Mich., 1961.

Offers a commendable treatment of Matthew 24 (285 pages).

The Gospel of Mark. William L. Lane, Eerdmans, Grand Rapids, Mich., 1974.

Offers a fairly comprehensive exposition of Mark's Olivet account (611 pages).

Matthew Henry's Commentary, Vol. 5. Matthew Henry, Revell, N.Y., N.Y.

Of limited value, and somewhat dated, but offers several key comments concerning portions of the Olivet prophecy.

The Gospel of Luke. William Hendriksen, Baker Book House, Grand Rapids, Mich., 1978.

His exposition on Chapter 21 is generally helpful (1082 pages).

The Gospel According to St. Mark. Alan Cole, Eerdmans, Grand Rapids, Mich., 1981.

His brief commentary on Chapter 13 is occasionally helpful (263 pages).

The Gospel According to Mark. G. Campbell Morgan, Revell, Old Tappan, New Jersey.

Provides a variety of constructive comments and insights into the Olivet prophecy (350 pages).

271

The Gospel According to Luke. G. Campbell Morgan, Revell, Old Tappan, New Jersey.

Provides a variety of constructive comments and insights into the Olivet prophecy (284 pages).

Evangelical Commentary on Mark. Ralph Earle, Zondervan, Grand Rapids, Mich., 1957.

His exposition of the Olivet prophecy considers a variety of prophetic perspectives (192 pages).

The Gospel According to St. Luke. Leon Morris, Eerdmans, Grand Rapids, Mich., 1974.

Occasionally helpful (345 pages).

The Gospel of Luke. Norval Geldenhuys, Eerdmans, Grand Rapids, Mich.

Occasionally helpful (670 pages).

General Bibliography

Barclay, William. *The Gospel of Luke.* Westminster Press, Philadelphia, Penn., 1975.

Beare, F. W. *The Gospel According to Matthew.* Harper & Row, San Francisco, Ca., 1981.

Blackstone, William E. *Jesus Is Coming.* Revell, Old Tappan, N.J., 1898.

Bloomfield, Arthur E. *Signs of His Coming.* Bethany Fellowship, Minneapolis, Minn., 1962.

Buswell, James D. *A Systematic Theology of the Christian Religion.* Zondervan, Grand Rapids, Mich., 1962.

Cairns, Earle E. *Christianity Through the Centuries.* Zondervan, Grand Rapids, Mich., 1954.

Conybeare, W. J. and Howson, J.S. *The Life and Epistles of St. Paul.* Eerdmans, Grand Rapids, Mich.

Cox, William E. *An Examination of Dispensationalism.* Presbyterian & Reformed Pub. Co., Philadelphia, Penn., 1971.

Dake, Finis Jennings. *Dake's Annotated Reference Bible.* Dake's Bible Sales, Inc., Laurenceville, Ga.

Durkin, Jim, et al. *The Coming World Crisis.* Radiance, Eureka, Ca., 1980.

Earle, Ralph. *Word Meanings in the New Testament, Vol. 1.* Beacon Hill Press, Kansas City, Mo., 1980.

Earle, Ralph, et al. *Beacon Bible Commentary, Vol. 6.* Beacon Hill Press, Kansas City, Missouri, 1964.

Earle, Ralph, et al. *Exploring the New Testament.* Beacon Hill Press, Kansas City, Missouri, 1968.

Eiselen, Frederick C., et al. *The Abingdon Bible Commentary.* Abingdon, Nashville, Tenn., 1927.

Ellicott, Charles John. *Ellicott's Bible Commentary.* Zondervan, Grand Rapids, Mich., 1971.

Eusebius, (Translated by Cruse, C.F.). *Ecclesiastical History.* Baker Book House, Grand Rapids, Mich., 1955.

Farquharson, James. *Daniel's Last Vision and Prophecy, Respecting Which Commentators Have Greatly Differed From Each Other, Showing Its Fulfillment in Events Recorded in Authentic History.* Aberdeen, Scotland, 1838.

Gaebelein, Arno C. *The Gospel of Matthew.* Loizeaux Brothers, Neptune, N.J., 1910.

Green, Jay P. *The Interlinear Bible, Vol. 4.* Baker Book House, Grand Rapids, Mich., 1979.

Guiness, H. Grattan. *The Approaching End of the Age.* Hodder & Stoughton, London.

Gundrey, Robert H. *The Church and the Tribulation.* Zondervan, Grand Rapids, Mich., 1973.

Guthrie, Donald. *Jesus the Messiah.* Zondervan, Grand Rapids, Mich., 1972.

273

Guthrie, Donald, et al. *The New Bible Commentary.* Revised, Eerdmans, Grand Rapids, Mich.

Hendriksen, William. *More Than Conquerors.* Baker Book House, Grand Rapids, Mich., 1940.

Ironside, H.A. *Lectures on Daniel the Prophet.* Loizeaux Brothers, Neptune, N.J., 1911.

Ironside, H.R. *Luke.* Loizeaux Brothers, Neptune, N.J., 1947.

Jamieson, Robert, et al. *Commentary on the New Testament, Vol. 1.* Revell, N.Y., N.Y.

Jones, Russell Bradley. *The Great Prediction of the Greatest Prophet* (Tract). Chapel Library, Venice, Florida.

Ladd, George. *The Blessed Hope.* Eerdmans, Grand Rapids, Mich., 1956.

Lahaye, Tim. *The Beginning of the End.* Living Books, Tyndale House Pub., Wheaton, Ill., 1981.

Lindsey, Hal. *The Late Great Planet Earth.* Zondervan, Grand Rapids, Mich., 1970.

Ludwigson, R. *A Survey of Bible Prophecy.* Zondervan, Grand Rapids, Mich., 1973.

Macpherson, Dave. *The Incredible Cover-Up.* Omega Pub., Medford, Oregon.

Mansel, Henry L. *The Gnostic Heresies of the 1st and 2nd Centuries.* AMS Press, N.Y., N.Y., 1875.

Mauro, Philip, *The Gospel of the Kingdom.* Reiner Pub., Swengel, Penn., 1978.

McCumber, William E. *Beacon Commentary on Matthew.* Beacon Hill Press, Kansas City, Missouri.

McKeever, Jim. *Christians Will Go Through the Tribulation.* Omega Pub., Medford, Oregon, 1978.

Morgan, G. Campbell. *Parables and Metaphors of Our Lord.* Revell, Old Tappan, New Jersey.

Morgan, G. Campbell. *Studies in the Four Gospels.* Revell, Old Tappan, New Jersey, 1927.

Newman, A.H. *A Manual of Church History, Vol. 1.* Judson Press, 1899.

Newton, Thomas. *Dissertations on the Prophecies, Vol. 2.* N.Y., N.Y., 1794.

Nicoll, W. Robertson. *The Expositors Bible, Vol. 5.* W.B. Ketcham Pub., N.Y., N.Y.

Pick, Aaron. *Dictionary of Old Testament Words.* Kregel Pub., Grand Rapids, Mich.

Plummer, Alfred. *The Gospel According to St. Mark.* Cambridge, The University Press, 1914.

Qualben, Lars P. *A History of the Christian Church.* Nelson, N.Y., N.Y., 1933.

Robertson. A.T. *Word Pictures in the New Testament, Vols. 1 and 2.* Broadman Press, Nashville, Tenn., 1930.

Ryrie, Charles C. *The Ryrie Study Bible.* Moody Press, Chicago, Ill., 1976.

Sanner, Elwood A. *Beacon Commentary on Mark.* Beacon Hill Press, Kansas City, Missouri.

Scofield, Cyrus I. *Scofield Reference Bible.* Oxford University Press, N.Y., N.Y., 1909.

Smith, Oswald J. *Is the Antichrist at Hand?* Christian Alliance Pub. Co., 1927.

Smith, William. *Smith's Bible Dictionary.* Zondervan, Grand Rapids, Mich., 1948.

Swete, Henry Barclay. *The Gospel According to St. Mark.* Macmillan & Co., London, England, 1952.

Thomas, Griffith. *St. Paul's Epistle to the Romans.* Eerdmans, Grand Rapids, Mich., 1946.

Thomas, Lawrence R. *Does the Bible Teach Millennialism?* Reiner Pub., Swengel, Penn.

Vine, W. E. *Expository Dictionary of New Testament Words.* Revell, Old Tappan, New Jersey.

Walvoord, John F. *Israel in Prophecy.* Zondervan, Grand Rapids, Mich., 1962.

Walvoord, John F. *Matthew: Thy Kingdom Come.* Moody Press, Chicago, Ill., 1974.

Welch, Reuben. *Beacon Commentary on Luke.* Beacon Hill Press, Kansas City, Missouri, 1974.

Wiersbe, Warren W. *Matthew - Meet Your King.* Victor Books, Wheaton, Ill., 1980.

Woodrow, Ralph. *His Truth is Marching On.* Riverside, Ca., 1977.

Wuest, Kenneth S. *The New Testament.* Eerdmans, Grand Rapids, Mich., 1981.

Wuest, Kenneth S. *Mark in the Greek New Testament.* Eerdmans, Grand Rapids, Mich., 1950.

Index of Subjects

Index of Scriptures